MW00984486

THE POWER
Of
WALKING
In
FORGIVENESS

My Life Story

Tamara J. Aycock

Paperback edition published 2019
ISBN 9781078492942

Printed in the United States of America

Dedication

First and foremost, I dedicate this book to God who formed me in my mother's womb, and who loved me no matter where I was at in my life.

To my friend Jesus, who stayed by my side and carried me through all the hard times in my life. He is the one who just loves spending time with me and me with Him. He never left me even in my darkest hour. The one I call my protector. The one who loved me so much, that He carried my sin on the Cross.

To Holy Spirit who has comforted me my whole life. Who teaches me and surrounds me with love. The One who keeps me going and shows me every direction to go (as long as I listen)!

I am thankful that God the Father, God the Son and God Holy Spirit gave me the time I needed to bring me to the place I am today. Without the Trinity in my life I would be nothing and I know I would not be on this earth if it was not for all three working in my life.

To my Daughter who has stayed by my side as I walked through this life even when I was away from God and with God. The one who has seen the good and bad side of me. The one who was there as I went through life changing inner healing. My one and only who did not give up on me as I tried to do the best with what I had to work with and forgave me of all the mistakes I made.

To my amazing Grandparents Warren and Lois Page from Rougemont, North Carolina, who loved me with unconditional love. The ones who spent hours and hours on their knees for me. The ones who showed me what a life was like living as a Christian. What it meant to stand and to KNOW God will see you through. My Grand-Daddy who went to Heaven before he was able to see the fruit of his prayers. My Grandma who NEVER turned her back on me and NEVER gave up on me! I can say that NEVER did I hear either one say one negative word to me not even when I was heart broken, disappointed or anything like that. They just gave me pure love.

To all my friends over the years who have been there holding my hand. Many for a season of life, some for the duration of time. I am thankful for each and every "crutch" God sent to me.

To all the people who have come from a place such as I have. Who are on a broken road searching for the flowers in the field of what I call life. I pray for inner healing for you. I pray for the strength and courage to forgive. I pray for FREEDOM from your past!

~Tamara J. Aycock

CONTENTS

1. Introduction..15
2. Six Miscarriages Then Me............................19
3. Changing The Last Name 48
4. Take Me, Let Him Live.................................70
5. Her Hands Were Cold..................................83
6. Let Him Die..99
7. You're Pregnant...116
8. Burnt Hands...127
9. I Didn't Know..130
10. He Never Left Me..140
11. You've Hurt Me..149
12. Holy Spirit Heal The Memories..................173
13. A Love Not Worth Finding.........................182
14. Double Rainbows.......................................191
15. Hold On This Is Going To Hurt..................202
16. Grandma's Final Gift..................................220
17. He Loved Me Enough To Send Crutches....226
18. Year Of Jubilee...231
19. The Cross...241
20. Wouldn't Change A Thing..........................246

ENDORSEMENTS

Tamara and I have been friends since we were 12. I think our brokenness brought us together as best friends.   Our friendship has been quite a crazy journey! This includes surviving being shot at and on another occasion of having a shotgun pulled on us. We put ourselves in situations that could have ended badly!! It's only by God's Grace that we survived all of this!

I was there to witness many of the heartaches Tamara lived through. She was there to pull me through some of the hardest times in my life. I'm happy to say that I am here to see where God has brought her. Her book touched my heart deeply. I feel strongly that it has the potential to help many on their own journeys of forgiveness.

Terri Burgess
Lifetime Best Friend

Tamara's story is filled with sadness, tragedy and redemption. Her book is life changing and offers hope and insight into a relationship with God, Jesus and the Holy Spirit. She shows us how the power of forgiveness can transform a life. If you know Tamara and don't know her story, you will find it hard to believe what life has thrown at her.

Tamara has walked through fire and has been refined into pure gold as only God can do. Because of the faith and prayers of her grandparents, she broke the cycle of a lifestyle that would have broken her much too soon. But through perseverance and not losing sight of the cross, she now partners with the Holy Spirit to show those in need how their lives can be transformed by the power of a loving God.

Pat Hillard
A good friend

Throughout her tragic life, one thing remained constant: God never left her.

This book chronicles the devastating events of Tamara Aycock's life as she journeys on the path God laid out for her.

You'll cry and then your heart will soar as you go from page to page, chapter to chapter learning what she endured during her lifetime.

While she prays for her readers, I pray that God always sends her double rainbows.

-Jennifer Bosk, President,
JRB Marketing/Media/Events

"If you forgive others the wrongs they have done to you, your Father in heaven will also forgive you." Matthew 6:14.

What an awesome God you serve. His plan and destiny for your life couldn't be silenced or stopped.

All that you encountered during your life's journey has been like clay in the potter's hand. You have developed into a remarkable woman who is constantly amazing me with your gifts and tenacity.

You are not afraid to tackle life and subdue obstacles in your way. Your book was an enjoyable experience. You can see and know people and have no idea what they have encountered in their lifetime. A young girl looking for love and getting her heart broken over and over again.

This book had me laughing and crying. I am sure that a lot of readers can relate or know someone who has gone through a similar ordeal. The same mistakes that many of us have made in life and kept quiet about, you also made and are courageous enough to share your most painful life experiences so others can be set free from shame and guilt and unforgiveness.

The revealing in your book will be a life changing experience for many. I agree with you that thousands will be blessed and set free by the power of the Word of God and your testimony. Love you and all that God has created you to be and that is a history maker in this earth. There are no limits on your talents and abilities to create and produce.

Barbara Best, Healing Rooms Team
And a Good, Good Friend.

Tamara Aycock's book, The Power of Walking in Forgiveness, presents her powerful testimony! I am undone as I read through the raw pain inflicted upon her innocence. I find myself crying as she pours out her experiences in these pages. Her once broken heart was the fruit of abuse and neglect, but through God's love and faithfulness – she is WHOLE!

I have known Tamara since 2011. I have witnessed her Christian life and I can testify that she truly is the overcomer that she declares in this book. Her life produces good fruit – ripe and ready for others to enjoy!

I have witnessed many of the miracles that she shares. God rescued His daughter! God alone gave her HOPE and RESTORATION!

May the God of hope fill you with all joy and peace as you trust in Him, so that you may overflow with hope by the power of the Holy Spirit. Romans 15:13

Tamara trusts in Him. I have seen her trust when times have been tough! Are you in a tough situation? Do you feel hopeless or need to see the light at the other end of the tunnel? God is faithful to bring you through! Tamara's life is a great example of perseverance and breakthrough! Her testimony will bring you HOPE.

You will be amazed at the offenses that Tamara (through Jesus) was able to lay down and overcome.

You too can overcome!   You too can experience breakthrough!

Get ready to begin your personal journey of healing and forgiveness as you read through these wonderful pages!   Tamara's encounters with miracles will stir up hope and expectation in your own life.   Her intimate relationship with the Father will create a hunger in your soul and make you want to press in for greater intimacy too!

May you walk in great healing, forgiveness, and revelation as you read this book.

God bless you mightily!
Beth K. Ferrell
Intercessor

The writing of 'The Power of Walking in Forgiveness; My Life Story'

I sent my testimony to a well-known TV ministry in the early 1990's. After several months, I received a letter in the mail explaining that my testimony was rejected because they believed no one could live through everything that I had experienced. After receiving that letter, I stopped talking about my past.

Beginning in 2012 until my book was printed; I had many prophetic words spoken over me about writing a book. Around the end of 2015 or early 2016, God gave me the title 'The Power of Walking in Forgiveness'. In the beginning I wasn't sure if He said "in" or "through". I asked again if it was "in" or "through" and also looked up the meaning of both words. Then I Knew I was supposed to use the word "in." See, when you walk through something you come out; it's not something you stay in. When you are walking in, you continue to stay in there. I knew that forgiveness is not a one-time thing; it is something you do whenever needed. I knew then my book was to be titled 'The Power of Walking IN Forgiveness My Life Story'.

I first began writing in the spring of 2017. While sitting at my desk waiting for my desktop computer to update, the power went out in the house. Losing power caused the computer to crash and a master reset had to be performed. There was no backup of my book, so I lost everything including the book. I rewrote the book and sent it to my editor, for her to review. Once she was done, she sent it back to me and then I realized I had left a lot of things out. I would wake up in the middle of the night and realized there were things I wanted to add to the book. I would get up, add it, then go back to sleep. After a few months of editing, I finally sent the "new book" back to the editor, around the beginning of 2019 and published on July 20, 2019. Writing this book has been a long process, but it was accomplished in God's timing, not mine.

$\underline{1}$
Introduction

Fix yourself a cup of hot tea and pull up a chair as we walk through these pages of ink of what I call my life in *The Power of Walking in Forgiveness.* I pray that as you turn the pages of my life, you may experience the presence of God in your life and Holy Spirit will bring healing in the areas you need healing in.

As you read, you will find I have been on many different roads some by choice and some were out of my control. For many years I lived with a broken heart and wearing a mask so no one would know what was really on the inside. I knew enough that I had to forgive people in order to be forgiven.

Through the years I thought that I had forgiven people who hurt me and I did but it was with words and not from my heart. It wasn't until I truly forgave from the heart the people in my life that had hurt me that things started to turn around in my life. I have found that many times in my life just because I had forgiven someone did not always mean I was healed of the hurt.

 Once you have truly forgiven someone and have been emotionally healed it will be like a scar on your body. You can remember how you got the injury and can see where it was but you cannot feel the pain anymore. Once you have forgiven someone and it's been healed you are able to look at that situation and not have any pain of the memory.

It was 1991, when God sent someone into my life for just a few minutes, that I was completely turned around. A person who I did not know and could not even identify their face to this day. A person who obeyed what God told them to do then walked out of the store that I was working in. A person who may never know what that one sentence spoke, how it totally changed my life. The stranger walked into the convenience store that I was working in to pay for gas. As I was ringing up the gas the person said to me "you are blaming God for everything that has happened in your life" then walked out the door. Under my breath I said "no I'm not". That day is the day God started showing me that I really was blaming Him. Once I realized what I was doing I knew in my heart that something had to change. I really did not want to keep living the way that I was. Being hurt, angry and mad at the world. Just living day by day and doing what I needed to do to get through the day. I didn't know how to change it but I knew something had to change. I was willing to do what I needed to do for the change to take place. That's when the true forgiveness started leading me into an inner healing in my heart from the years of pain that I had carried and covered up.

In a sense I had to give up my right in order to forgive. See I had the right to be hurt. I had the right to be upset. I had many rights due to the things that were done to me but I couldn't forgive when I was holding on to my rights.

Let's journey down this once broken road together and see how God turned the ashes into beauty and it all started with me willing to forgive.

2
Six Miscarriages Then Me

This chapter is what I would call the hardest part of my life and the hardest to even write. My Mom and I have had a very distant relationship as Mom and Daughter. I have tried over and over to have a relationship with her for it to always end up the same. She is a broken woman who wants to live in all the pain of her life not wanting to let go and forgive. She has become a bitter very negative person. Her pain comes out in her words and actions to others especially me. My Mom's life is a reflection every day in my life of why I had to forgive not once but time after time. I never wanted to become the person my Mom is so I chose to walk in forgiveness.

Growing up as a young child I remember my Mom and Grandma telling me often how hard my Mom and Dad tried to have a child. Mom kept having miscarriages and then on the seventh time she did not miscarry and had a baby girl which would be me. Through the years it really did not seem that important in my life until I was in my adult Christian life. Walking down the broken road in my life I had to remind myself many times that I was child number seven and God had a plan for me and it was a plan for good and not destruction. Number seven means completion in the Bible. I never asked my Mom if she thought she would miscarry with me or not. Maybe after six she lost hope and thought her seventh pregnancy would end up like in the past, a miscarriage. But baby number seven would go full term and be born.

Overall, I don't recall a time when my Mom and I were close at all. As far back as I can remember I spent more time with my Grandparents than my Mom. Remembering back to the age of around seven I don't recall times of my Mom telling me she loved me or even sitting me in her lap or anything of that sort. I don't recall her giving me any affection or speaking words like I love you.

However, I do remember the day when I was around seven possibly just turned eight. It was a sunny day and I decided to walk to my friend's house up the street. This is something that I did often when spending the night with my Grandparents. Before leaving the house I decided to take a frozen grape Kool-Aid in that little famous yellow cup Grandma always made for me. It had rained earlier and water was running through the ditch so I decided that I would walk in the ditch and let the water run over my feet. Nothing usual for this child to do. But that day something was different I stepped on something and it hurt really bad. I pulled up my right foot to find my big toe cut almost off, it was only attached by a small piece of skin. I was bleeding pretty badly. I made it to my friend's house being it was closer than my Grandparents and they called 911 and my Grandma. Then Grandma called my Mom and before long my Mom was pulling in that driveway so fast that she turned the car sideways coming in. She was pregnant with my brother and the EMS workers took her keys right there. I remember being in the ambulance when she got there and thought even at such a young age that she really did love me. If she didn't she wouldn't have been so upset that I almost cut my toe off. I made it to the hospital and got more stiches than a kid would want. I often think about that day for some reason. Maybe it's because that was the one day that I can remember that my Mom showed she loved me. Something had happened to me and she wanted to get to me.

A few days later going back to my Grandparents and my toe was healing, I walked back to that place to see what I had stepped on. Turns out someone had thrown out a glass drink bottle and it had broken, and I had stepped on the jiggered part of the bottle. It was only by God's grace and His healing power that I was able to keep my big toe. Had my toe been completely cut off the toe would have flowed down stream in the ditch and I would have lost my big right toe.

A few months later when I was eight years old my brother was born and Mom had a very bad experience during birth and almost died. This was her eighth pregnancy with only two babies making it full term. I don't know the details and I never asked what happened. I just know it was bad.

At a few weeks old my brother got sick with yellow jaundice and he almost died. He was in the hospital for a long time. Something happened at this time and it was like Mom threw me out the window and her focus was just on my brother. I could understand it while he was sick however it continued even after he was well. There was a bond between them that was inseparable. Not long after my brother was born Mom married my brother's Dad and we seemed to be a normal happy family. I was happy to have a Dad. I missed my real Dad so much so having someone to call Dad was good. I thought I would have someone who would love me also. As you will read in another chapter that wasn't the case. This was my Mom's third marriage before age 30. Her first marriage was my biological Dad. Second marriage was to a man that only lasted a few months. From what I remember he treated her well and she told me she left the marriage because he did not wash his face. I'm not too sure that is the real reason why the marriage failed. Her third marriage was to my brother's Dad. After a third marriage she lived with a man for 30 years.

What little relationship my Mom and I had at this point started going down and down. Such a young age of eight I remember feeling like I wasn't even noticed around the house. Many times my Mom would start yelling at me for this or that. Do this, do that or get me this. I remember a day when I was around eight or nine I had gotten in trouble again and was sent to my safe heaven, sorry I mean my bedroom. I was so upset and so hurt that I wanted to have nothing to do with my Mom again. So many emotions for a little girl. I laid on my bed not wanting to get under the covers because I felt like they were not mine but hers. She bought them so they pretty much were hers. I used my winter coat to cover up with. To me that was mine and I felt safe and comfortable under it. I was so warm and comfortable that I fell asleep. When I woke up my coat was gone and I went to ask my Mom where my coat was. She told me she washed it. I never asked her why she did that I just took it as a love act. To this day I have never bought that up in a conversation. Was it truly a love act or was it her taking the only thing that I felt was mine. This question I will never know the answer as I will never ask her for the truth.

As I left my childhood years and moved into teenage years our relationship became more and more distant. We started fighting and totally not getting along. To me no matter what I did, I could not do anything right in her eyes and this is pretty much still the same today. The distance from my Mom and not having my "real" Dad in my life and now a "step" Dad who was doing things to me that should not be done caused deep wounds in me. Heart breaking mornings of my step Dad coming into my bedroom to wake me up to go to school. As time went, by this increased to his hands moving from touching my butt to wake to up to moving up my legs into my private areas. Then it progressed to his body parts into my body parts. (I will go into more details about my step dad and my relationship in a later chapter.) My Mom is in the house and never noticed or just didn't say anything. She never questioned why he started waking me up for school. I turned to smoking cigarettes as soon as I turned 16. Then drinking and that turned into drugs. I used things to cover the pain in my life and what was going on. My life was really becoming a nightmare and substance abuse was my way to handling it.

Days, months and years went on and the once arguments had now turned into fights between my Mom and I. When I was at home I stayed in my bedroom to stay away from her. So many times I could hear her and my "step" Dad fighting and them hitting each other. There was this one time that I came out of my room and went to the kitchen and yelled at both of them. I begged them to stop fighting or I was going to call 911. At that time my step Dad turned to me and came after me. He had me pinned in the corner with the table in front of me and then I saw my Mom pick up a kitchen chair and hit him in the head to get him away from me. I thought go Mom, thanks for your help! It was not often my Mom would take my side she would rather hang tight with a man who ran around on her, didn't care anything about her and treated her like nothing. To his credit, he did work hard and paid the bills at the house while my life was becoming a living nightmare living under the same roof with him.

I had just started driving and Mom let me use her car to learn to drive. It was a straight drive (or manual stick) and I had never drove one before. Well the one thing you always want to tell someone who is learning to drive a straight drive you MUST press the clutch and the brake at the same time to stop! That part was skipped in my lesson and as I drove into the driveway the car did not stop and there I was running into our trailer! No big deal it was my bedroom at the front. I forgot to hit the clutch and the brake. Thankfully where was no damage to Mom's car or the trailer!

The older I got the fights and arguments between my Mom and I continued and it seemed I was always getting in the middle of her and my step Dad fighting. My go to place to get away was to go outside and sit under the back on our trailer. So many times I sat on that cold, damp dirt crying my eyes out with what was going on. That was the place where I thought about taking my life but scared to do so because I didn't want to go to hell. I was raised to believe that if a person took their life they would go to hell. That was the place where I talked to God about why I was born and why would He allow all this to happen to me if He loved me. That was the place where I started to believe that God didn't love me at all and I was born for nothing. I only had one person to talk to and that was my best friend Terri. We were going through a lot of the same things so our bond was based on traveling down the same road. This was at the same time things were happening with my stepdad that I could not tell anyone. Terri was the one and only person I trusted enough to talk to. I told Terri a lot of things but some I choose to keep to myself. I spent countless hours just talking to God. At that time I wasn't sure if He heard me but just telling Him what I thought and asking a lot of questions. I felt very empty on the inside, useless and actually lost of hope. I didn't see a future for me. I just lived day to day and did what I needed to do to get through the day.

Many times I had to remember I was baby number seven based on the miscarriages. I was so back and forth with my life and my future. I had no dreams for the future. How does one dream when you don't even believe in yourself? Drugs helped me so much at least I thought they did at the time. I got to where I could not function without them. Being high I didn't think about the pain and hurt I was living with every day. They made me feel numb and helped me to escape the reality of what was going on in my life. I grew up with what I would call no love or support from my Mom. When I was at home I stayed in my bedroom and she on the couch watching TV. I didn't want to fight or argue with her so I stayed away. Often times I would sneak out at night and go to a party or just to get high. Trying the best I could to deal with things by covering up the pain.

Then came graduation and time to move out of Mom's. I didn't go wild I was already wild before I moved out. I was one partying girl that was broken inside and out trying to find what life was all about. I had gotten pregnant and married so now Mom wasn't just Mom she was Grandma as well. As time went by time proved my Mom was the same to my daughter as she was to me. Protecting my daughter I did not allow her to spend the night or spend much time with my Mom. I had made a promise I would never be the Mom to my daughter as my Mom was to me and I kept that promise. I would not allow my Mom any chance to speak negative words to my daughter so I kept her away from her.

After my divorce and then my Mom's divorce my Mom and I found ourselves living under the same roof again. This time it was a little different and our relationship was somewhat on the mends to where we could talk. We started going to bars together and hanging out as well. It seemed that the road I was going down was one and the same my Mom had gone down. Here I was 21, a Mom, and divorced and raising a daughter. Same road - two different people. My Mom and I never talked about the past just two people who lived every day covering up the pain from yesterday. Two different people on two different paths but yet the same path. How ironic. Neither road by choice but the circumstances of life caused our paths that we were on. A Mom and Daughter by blood but total strangers in the natural with a common bond of heartache and brokenness. Neither of us knowing what the other person was like nor what we even liked other than drinking. For me drinking covered up the past, killed the pain of today and numbed the future. My Mom going to bars, used friends and boyfriends to help with her pain. Never a word of I'm sorry or I love you just connected by virtue of family ties.

In 1986 I had met a guy and only wanted to be friends. He wanted to date but I knew he was not the one for me. He kept hanging around the house and Mom started dating him. This guy caused so much drama and stress in our small little family. He would start fights with me and my brother. I ended up moving out of the house with my daughter. This man was really important to her. So important that she ended up leaving our family and not coming to any subsequent family functions with my Grandparents, my Aunt or myself. In addition I did not allow her to see her one and only grandchild. She started lying just as he did. You could never trust a word that came out of her mouth. Neither one of them wanted to work or would pay their bills. They were always moving from place to place. My mom would go months without anyone hearing from her then out of the blue she would call. For the most part her phone calls were to cuss me out then hang up on me or ask for money.

This was around the same time God started doing a huge work in me. He started showing me things in my life that had to change in order for me to be able to move forward. One thing was I had to forgive my Mom in order to move on. God wanted me to forgive my Mom, so I could be healed for all the pain and hurt she has caused in my life. I really didn't want to forgive her. I did not think she deserved to be forgiven. God told me to write a letter to my Mom. I did and I pour out my broken heart in the pages explaining my hurt to her. As I wrote, God healed my broken heart. Through the years I continued to try to have a relationship with my Mom. When a person is heartbroken they lash out in their pain to hurt others. To this day I still put my heart on the line trying but yet that wall is still up with her.

As time went on it became obvious with Mom and Daughter we were really on two different paths. Her path was with a boyfriend, my path was with God. I had grown up going to church with my Grandparents so I knew God, but I just didn't know him in a personal way. Once I was able to know Jesus and not just in name only is when a tremendous healing occurred, and forgiveness began. It seemed my Mom loved pushing those buttons and testing my walk with God. She would call and cuss me out about this or that then hang up on me. I tell you it was HARD! Her calls got so bad that I had to block her and her boyfriend phone numbers so she could not call me.

I had been Grandma's power of attorney for about 10 years and my Mom had a problem with that. My Mom was upset through the years feeling she should have been Grandma's power of attorney, she was the oldest and I was the grandchild. My Mom went years without seeing my Grandma, her Mother. Days and months without calling but yet she wanted to be the power of attorney! Little did my Mom know she was the reason my grandma chose to have a power of attorney! I remember the day I had to call Mom to tell her Grandma had died. That is the same time I took the block off my phone so Mom could call me again. I knew because of my Mom's actions and not spending time with my Grandma for twenty five years before she passed away that my Mom was going to have some regrets. It had been over a year since Mom seen Grandma and once she got the phone call from me reality would be she would not be able to talk to her or see her alive anymore.

I remember after Grandma's service Mom calling me and telling me I had done a good job with her service. Now that was the first time Mom told me something good in years! That is the day I believe that things started changing with my Mom. I believe with all my heart part of my Mom's problem with me was she was jealous of the relationship I had with my Grandma. Conversations started flowing again, still not talking about the past just, day to day. My Mom was still living with her boyfriend and he still tried to continue to stir up stuff with us. Things were a lot different this time versus the past. I had a relationship with God so I was able to let things go and not get upset. In my heart, I knew there would be a day I would get a call from my Mom and she would need me. I just knew it. It came May 2014, when the guy she had lived with for 30 years left her for a woman who was my age and was my Mom's best friend. My mom had been a better Mom to this woman than she was to me. That was the day when my heart broke for my Mom. All her life, everything she loved had hurt her. That was the same time I asked God to show me my Mom through His eyes. That is the same day I had also seen a young broken little girl. It broke my heart to see my Mom through the eyes of Jesus and see the pain and how broken she was. When I got that call I loaded up my car with cleaning supplies and took off to my Mom's house. That day I told my Mom that I was sorry that she had been left alone. I told her I was sorry that she had been hurt so much. If I could I would take all that from her, I would. I told her I was sorry she had to go through this. In response my Mom asked me forgive her. I said yes, Mom I did that years ago. Then she asked even for hitting you in your face? I said yes, Mom, even for that, years ago. My Mom had hit me in my face when I was sixteen. For all these years she had carried the pain of that without telling me.

Once I got to her place, I saw that it was unfit for my dog to even live there. I spent 10 hours cleaning a kitchen and living room. She had no hot water, no running toilet, no heat, no food and she was living in just one room of the house. I tell you it broke my heart. No matter what she had ever done to me she was my Mom and I had forgiven her and I was going to help her. My brother could not help her because his life was in the same place mine had been years ago – mired in pain and hurt.

I guess once you look through the eyes of Jesus you don't look with eyes of judgment and you can truly see.

Perhaps the strange tie between my Mom and I was created when I was a child with feelings of not being loved after my brother was born. I'm sure when you almost die giving birth and then the child almost dies it would create a bond that is unbreakable. However, I never really understand why my Mom favored my brother when he was into the things he was and he never held onto a job even to this day.

I, on the other hand have worked hard my whole life and everything I have gotten I've gotten by working.

Then, one day, a few years back, it was like a light bulb came on in my head. Could it be my Mom felt like I did not need her the way my brother does?

Years later after everything was said and done, I can look back and see the pain my Mom carried because of her third husband doing the things he did to me. I'm sure that is a pain that is sharper than a knife in the heart and one that is not easily removed.

I have also thought, could it be that I remind my Mom of my Dad and looking at me brings back the pain of a divorce. Kind of crazy that so many years later when she spoke of him I could tell she still loved him. Even to this day, 53 years after the divorce. The few times I was able to see or talk to my Dad I also knew he still loved her. They never spoke of why they divorced and I never asked. It happened when I was a very young child and I never remembered them being together.

The fourth man who she lived with for 30 years but never married was not a working man. Many times, they asked for handouts and it got to a point that I had to say I could not give them any more money to help them. I was single raising a Daughter and trying to pay for my own bills. While I was never rich, as they thought I was I also struggled to pay my bills and I worked a lot of hours to do so. When they called asking for money I simply said I don't have it. The asking got so often I had to make the decision to stop taking away from my own bills to help them while they sit at home watching TV and I worked two jobs.

My Brother is still in the same place in terms of how he handles things and my Mom now lives in the same boarding house he does. My Mom still lives with all the pain and hurt of the past by not forgiving and letting go. Still to this day she will tell me, I don't know how you forgive him for what he did to you. I can't. I know she is referring to my stepdad.

As I stated earlier, my Mom and I were two different people on two different paths that lead to the same place of pain and hurt. The difference between my life and my Mom's is I chose to forgive which then took me to a different road and a different place in my life. I don't know if my Mom will get to a place where she will forgive so that she can be released from the pain and hurt. But I do know this, if you are not able to forgive you cannot move on and you will carry the pain of what happened until forgiveness is accomplished. Not with just words but truly forgive from the heart. I do pray that one day my Mom will be able to do so.

For her just like it was for me years ago, love equals pain, so it's better to not love than to feel the pain again. Those years I chose not to love were during the years I was a broken woman. When God healed my heart I was able to love even myself. The truth is once you are at that point of brokenness you are not able to carry the love of Jesus nor accept his love. For me I was not able to accept the fact that Jesus loved me when I felt like no one else loved me and I didn't love myself. One may ask, how does one know that to be true? I would say from my life experience of wearing the mask. For years people would say I love you and I would respond I love you. The truth was I did love them with my words but in my heart I didn't. I did not know what love was or how to give love at that point and time in my life. Love for me was pain and I tried everything to stay away from pain. I wouldn't let anyone get close to me that way my heart would not get broken again.

Mom lived in that run down house for two years. Day after day I tried to get her to move out since it had no hot water, nonworking toilet, only one electric outlet that would work no stove, broken windows and five feet of water in the basement. She would not move; it was her home she said. She had only been there two months before I got that call he (her boyfriend) had left. I guess she was tired of moving. It seemed they had moved every year.

All that time I was faithful in doing Mom's clothes, keeping her house clean, taking her to the doctor and doing her shopping. She would not leave the house except for the doctor.

That house was the place of her pain. She suffered even more pain than that was caused by the man she was with for 30 years, leaving her for her best friend. The same woman who had babysat my Daughter, the same woman who my Mom raised as a child of her own. The same woman who owned the house my Mom and her boyfriend moved into. The same woman who my Mom loved more than me. It was her place of pain and she was not going to move out and move on from that pain.

Then that one day I got the call from the "other woman" she said Mom had to move. I couldn't believe my ears she still called my Mom "Mom". The woman who was living with my Mom's boyfriend still calls her Mom! My Mom still allowed her to call her Mom. I said "no problem", I can do this I said to myself! My Mom ended up moving into the same boarding house where my Brother lived.

She had three dogs and five cats and finding a place to move with the animals and her low income was hard. I had offered her to come live with me, however, she could not smoke in my house and she refused. Once Mom was moved she gave my Brother her SSI card and food stamp card. So for two years he took care of her needs since they lived in the same house. I still stayed in contact with her and visited; however, her basic needs my Brother was now making sure were met.

Then in October 2016, I got that call I never thought I would get. Tammy I have to talk to you! I could hear it in her voice. "I have not eaten in three days!, Mom's voice came across the airwaves telling me my Brother had not been taking care of her and she was hungry and had not eaten in three days. I was at her house within 15 minutes! I got both of her cards and now I am back taking care of her. I have noticed in the past two months my Mom saying I love you every time before she hangs up. My heart sinks as I hear those words because I know that she is doing the best she can and she really does love me. It's not just words but it's all she can give. But yet I struggle to say I love you back.

During this time with God's help I have moved from a place of taking care of my Mom because she is my Mom no matter what, to I really do want to take care of her.

A few years ago someone came up to me and spoke these words to me "Your Mom is acting the way she is because of a broken heart." I will never forget those words. The words were spoken out of the mouth of a person who had no clue as to who I was but they were someone God used to speak those words. Fast forward to today, my Mom's health is not the best so she requires more care than some at her age and I honestly want to help.

For the most part, my Mom has really no desire to live. She just lives each day with no dreams, no goals and no desire for anything only brokenness. When a person lives in that state it can also bring in depression. If only she would get to a place where she could walk in forgiveness and release the pain and hurt of the past. For me, I can look at the road my Mom is on and where she has been and know that I could very well be on that same road had God not entered into my life with an over whelming push to forgive. Because of this, I am able to walk in forgiveness and live life to the fullest in my Heavenly Dad while at the same time being the only bright light to my Mom. Making sure to remind her that the past is the past. I forgive you, I love you and you are my Mom and nothing can take that away from you or me.

It was a Sunday afternoon on February 3, 2013, as I drove down Highway 85 looking for a place to stop for lunch. I had seen a billboard for Cracker Barrel so I decided I would go there. Once off the exit I wasn't able to find the side road to enter into Cracker Barrel parking lot so I ended up going to KFC. Not a favorite place to go but one that I could get in eat and back on the road. I wasn't sure why but I felt God had a purpose for me to go to that KFC. Once I entered into the restaurant I went to the bathroom. I heard the toilet running water so me being me I lifted the water tank lid off to jiggle the handle to see if the water would stop running. Once I did that I heard Holy Spirit say that is how I am always to flow through you no blockage. I was kind of like, okay Holy Spirit but couldn't you have shown that to me at Cracker Barrel instead of here? Then I went to order my food and I heard a song that I knew from back in the day. As I ate I recalled the words "she never called to say I love you". As I heard those words I said God I hope my Mom doesn't say that about me. I knew once I got in my car I needed to call my Mom. As I walked outside

45

there were two women standing outside and I heard one say I don't think she cares. I tell you I turned around real quick because it sounded just like my Mom's voice. As soon as I got in my car I called my Mom. I told her I do love her even though we don't talk much. I don't know why he choose KFC for the place to show me this. Perhaps it's because KFC was my Grandma's favorite place to go. I just knew what I had to do because I did not want my Mom to leave the face of this earth believing that I did not love or care about her. With everything put to the side she was still my Mom. That is the day that God started moving in our relationship but it took me obeying and receiving from the experience He sent to get my attention. God knows how to talk to me for me to get things done. Using that song got my attention! After the phone call I remembered the song correctly. The real words were I just called to say I love you. But that is not what I heard initially. If it had been the original words to the song, it would not have gotten my attention. God knows what it takes to get His kids' attention.

Still to this day as my book is coming near the end to be published, my Mom and I still struggle. I keep trying to help her but I keep getting rejected. She is very mean to me and rejects everything I try to do when all I am trying to do is help her. She still calls and hangs up and says things to try to hurt me. I have been told over and over by friends to stop helping her. Stop putting yourself out there for her to keep trying to tear you down. My mind wants to but my heart tells me no. She is my Mom and to be honest I am the only one that can help her. She needs me even though she hurts me almost daily by making sure to say that what I do is not good enough. But I continue on. I pray that one day it will change before she leaves the face of this earth. While I have great faith, this situation looks impossible in the natural, but then I am reminded with God all things are possible.

3
Changing the Last Name

In this chapter you will read about the heart break of my life not having my biological Dad as part of my life. The pain I felt with my Dad was something completely different than that of my Mom. My Dad was an absent Dad which created a void in my heart. The longing to get to know and be with my Dad. It wasn't about forgiveness with my Dad per se; it was more about the pain and hurt of him not being a part of my life. While I had to forgive my Dad of some thing's, it was more about my broken heart needing inner healing instead of forgiveness.

Growing up without my biological Dad was very hard on me even into my adult years. My parents divorced when I was real young and I have no memory of them being together. I knew the story of how they met. He worked on trees in his younger years and my Mom met him while working near my Grandparents house. They met, got married, and had me after six miscarriages. I was told from a young age my Dad lived in another state and my Aunt Mae on my Dad's side lived on the same road as my Mom's parents, my grandparents. My Grandma Aycock also lived with my Aunt Mae.

Through the years, my Dad showed he had no interest in me and stayed out of the picture except a few short visits maybe once a year or every two years. Honestly the only thing I knew about him was his name and birth month and day. My Grandma Aycock was very pleasant to me and treated me like family but never showed love towards me.

After my parents divorce my Dad became an over the road truck driver who lived in West Virginia, South Carolina and then Virginia. There were very few occasions my Dad would come to North Carolina to see me. I remember one time he came in and he bought me a jewelry box in the shape of a bird house. I loved it so much; it was light blue and the first gift that I remember getting from him. His visits were always short - very short and my heart was torn watching him leave again. I would watch him leave not knowing when I would see him again. Amazing that I loved him so much but yet didn't know him at all. The truth is he was my Dad and his girl loved him.

Another time I remember him coming to see me was during school break. My Mom let me go with him and his girlfriend Helen over the road in his tractor trailer. I really liked Helen and she liked me and we got along great. Truth be known I saw my Dad a lot more during the time he was dating her. I was excited to be able to spend time with him and Helen. To this day I remember how excited I was. Off we went and then once we were in the mountains the excitement changed to fear! He scared the daylights out of me going down that mountain. I thought that truck was going to go off the side of the mountain! Knowing my Dad had been driving a truck for years and years didn't help that little heart of mine to remain calm. He knew how to roll and drive that truck and I had seen him put that thing in places I never thought it could go. He knew what he was doing and his experience showed it. My Dad noticed that the trailer had a small leak and he had to have it fixed before we could load up. Because of the leak repair I was going to be gone longer than expected and that I packed for. I ran out of underwear. Dad and Helen took me to K-mart to buy me underwear. Something like that may seem like a small thing but to this girl it was huge. It was my first time going shopping with my Dad. I was super happy to spend time with my Dad. I was in heaven on earth. Then it was time for me to go back home. My heart broke as I watched him leave me again. I knew it would be a long time before I would see or hear from him again, if I did. Reality was this little girl needed her Dad really bad and it hurt for him not to be around me.

I missed my Dad so much and often thought it would be better to have a Dad who had died instead of one who didn't want to have anything to do with me. It really hurt me and caused a lot of issues during my teenage years and young adult life. I often felt like no one would want me. If my Dad didn't why would someone else? I often thought why would he not want to spend time with me since I was his only daughter? I was actually his only child. Why did he not love me? What was wrong with me? I loved him and he was my Dad and yet he did not want to even call me. I just didn't understand it at all. Years and years went by and more and more pain built up in my heart. I told my Mom I thought he must have died. I didn't understand how he could be alive and not want to come see me. I guess my Mom felt bad for me, but she was able to get in touch with him. I don't know how but she was able to always get in touch with him.

My Mom got in touch with my Dad and told him that I didn't have a car. He made a trip to come see me and bought me a car. It was an old police car and even had a TV in it. I was one happy girl to have a car but that car didn't take the place of my Daddy being gone. I didn't have the car long either because I made the mistake of telling my Mom that car would run 100 MPH! The next thing I knew my Dad came back and took that car! My mom had called him and told him. Hey truth be known I got my lead foot from him! Looking back I guess that was a good thing but at that time it broke my heart. He gave me something and then came and took it back. I didn't look at it like he was saving my life or saving me from possibly being in a wreck.

A couple of years later, in 1983, my Mom got in touch with him again and he came to see me. I was pregnant, getting or either just got married. Again he came with gifts: a crockpot and a set of yellow Tupperware canisters. I still have the gifts to this day - 36 years later. Then off he went again and it would be years and years before I would see him again.

When I got married to my daughter's Dad I was most excited about changing my last name from Aycock to my husband's last name. I hated the last name Aycock. Every time I had to tell someone my last name or hear them call me Tamara Aycock it bought all that pain back to me of my Dad not being around. I could not get away from the pain.

In 1987, after I had an abortion, my Mom's boyfriend started a bunch of stuff about me telling everyone I had AIDS. At that point, I knew I needed to get out of town and fast. I was going to kill that man if I didn't. I'm just telling you the truth I would have killed him! I was a woman full of pain and brokenness at that time. I didn't care about nothing but my daughter and grandparents.

Somehow I found my Dad's phone number and called him. He invited me to come to South Carolina with my Daughter and live with them. Talking about something being very hard to do, leaving my Grandparents in NC. Two people who I loved so dearly and would not be able to see again until I came back to NC. I also had to talk to my daughter's Dad who would also not to get to see his daughter. As hard as the decision was I knew the only way to fill the void in my heart and get to know my Dad was to go to South Carolina. This would also give my daughter a chance to get to know her Granddaddy and him her. I got a ticket for us on Greyhound Bus to Columbia, South Carolina and off we went. Once there, I got to meet his wife and her daughters. Initially things were going well in South Carolina. I was getting along with my Dad and his family. Plus I met a guy and started dating him. It felt kind of like starting all over again leaving North Carolina and all the problems and mess. I felt like I could breathe again and breathe deep fresh air. The only thing I missed were my grandparents!

Then one day my Dad found a pregnancy test under the master bathroom sink. He came to me believing that it was mine. I told him that it was not mine! I tried to convince him I was telling the truth but he would not listen to me. I could not bring myself to tell him that I had an abortion right before I came to live with them so there was no way that I would sleep with a guy, I would not take that chance of getting pregnant. I was heartbroken when he told me I needed to leave. Heartbroken! I tried to convince him I was telling the truth but he would not listen to me. I called my cousin from North Carolina who drove down to get my daughter and me. My Dad would not even buy us a bus ticket to get back to North Carolina. More knives in my heart from my Dad.

I don't recall exactly but I believe the next time I would see my Dad was in 1990 after moving back from South Carolina was when Mom got in touch with him again to come see me. I guess the message of that phone call was your Daughter is dying and you need to come see her before she checks out of this world. During this time my liver was shutting down. I had been diagnosed with cirrhosis of the liver. However, it turned out that all the medical problems were coming from my gallbladder and not my liver. By the time my Dad was able to get to me I had already had emergency surgery and gotten out of the hospital. My grandparents took me to their house so they could take care of me and my daughter. Again his visit was very short but I believe he stayed a couple of days that time. I don't recall too much because I was recovering and it's hard to remember anything.

Then there was that time I got a call about a year later; I remember my Mom telling me my Dad was really sick and was at my Aunt Mae's. My Grandma Aycock lived with Aunt Mae so Dad would stop by to see his Mom. I drove over to my Aunt Mae's house to see my Dad. As a young adult, that day I walked into that house and saw my Daddy laying on the couch. It was a real heartbreaking time for me. There was my Daddy, the one that I really loved, who had never been there for me, dying from black lung disease. As a young adult woman and a woman who had a lot of brokenness and pain in me - I'm sure I said a little prayer to God for him. But a prayer I really didn't think God would hear or answer. I did not think God loved me, or cared too much for me, or hear my prayers. But that didn't stop me from praying. The absence of my Daddy caused me to have a spirit of rejection and orphan spirit. A sprit of rejection is feeling as through everyone will reject you. An orphan spirit is feeling you were never loved or wanted. At that time, I did not know what either one of those spirits were nor did I know I had them. All I knew was I had a lot of heart break! I got word that my Dad pulled through and was going to live.

My Aunt Mae lived on the same road as my grandparents on my Mom's side. So many times I went down Ross Road and look at my Aunt's houses wondering if my Dad was there and I did not know it. For that part of the family they never accepted me into the family or as his daughter. They treated me well but not as a family member. When my Grandma Aycock was alive she was the one who stayed on my Dad about making visits to see me even the few times he did. I got the call that my Grandma Aycock had died and I prepared myself to go to her service. Once she died my Dad's visits stopped. In my eyes, even a visit once a year or every two years was better than nothing at all.

In 1991 when God started doing an inner healing in me, my Dad was part of it; however, I still carried the issues of pain from the spirit of rejection and the orphan spirit. A spirit of rejection causes a person to stay distant from people. You reject people before they have a chance to reject you. For me that was a "safe zone," I would not let people get close to me so I would not get hurt again. The orphan spirit causes a person to feel alone, not wanted and not accepted. I had forgiven my Dad but still had the pain of his absence everywhere I went.

Fast forward to 2003, when I got married for the second time and somehow I found my Daddy through a switchboard. All the years of hurting, all the years of longing to see him, all the years of pain and the hurt of him not being around; he was still my Dad and I loved him and missed him. When I called his wife answered the phone. I didn't want her to know it was me on the phone, so I asked to speak to Ted, she asked who was calling I said Tammy. She said he doesn't have anything to give you. I told her I don't want anything from him. I just wanted to talk to him. I didn't understand her telling me that since I have never asked him for anything, not one thing in my whole life! Then she put him on the phone.

I talked to him a few minutes. I told him that I owned my own company, owned a house and was married. I ask if I could come see him and he said yes. I told him over and over Daddy I don't want anything from you just you. You are my Daddy and I love you. I told him I would call in a couple of days to get the directions to come see him.

At that time he was living in Covington, Virginia, and when I called two days later the phone was disconnected. Another knife right to the heart. How could it be that you long to be with someone and you allow them over and over to hurt you and yet you still keep pursuing a relationship with them? My Dad has always been on my mind through the years always wondering where he is, is he alive, what is he doing.

As life went on, even in the absence of my Daddy my mind always stayed on him. A few years passed when I googled his name as I often do, and I found out his wife had died. I guess they had moved and again his number was a public number so you know I had to call. He answered the phone and I talked to him. I told him I was sorry his wife had died. He asked how I got his number and I told him switchboard and he told me he did not know what that was. He also told me something that took the last piece of my heart. He said "if I knew it was you I would not have answered the phone". You talking about crushing a person those words did more than anything. See I couldn't blame it on his wife she wasn't alive anymore I had to look at my Dad and realize it was him and only him that didn't want to see me. If I had been his wife not wanting me around, he would have taken the opportunity to see me but, it was him! He even told me he would rather be by himself. CRUSHED!

Not long after the conversation with my Dad, I found myself, 14 months later, saying I do to he don't and yes, he left the marriage. Again I was crushed When it came to the divorce in 2005 I was driven by pain. I did not want to carry Scarth as my last name because that was huge amount of pain and I could not go back to Aycock because that was pain.

I called my daughter's dad and told him I wanted to go back to Clemons and if the judge did not allow me to go back to his last name (my daughter's father) he would have to divorce his wife, remarry me, to give me his last name again - then he could go back to his wife.

Both the last name Scarth and Aycock had a lot of pain that went with them so I just could not have them as my last name anymore. I did not want to be reminded every day of the pain of not having my Dad around nor the pain of the divorce by carrying my ex-husband's last name Scarth. I did not want to go through life with a painful last name. Even though my daughter's Dad and I were divorced, not once did he ever hurt me or cause me pain! Our divorce was due to me being a broken young woman who could not receive love. I did what a broken person does, I rejected the person that loved me before he could hurt me. Looking back I know that he would have never hurt me and our marriage would have lasted. The divorce was on my side. As a result, I could live with being called by his last name Clemons because there wasn't any emotional pain involved other than birthing our child - now that was a lot of pain! The judge granted me to go back to the last name Clemons.

Ten years later, February 2015, I was sitting in my lazy boy when God spoke to me and said you are living in a false identity and need to go back to your roots, your inheritance. I was like what? What are you talking about? I just didn't get it. Then he started showing me. I was carrying the last name Clemons and I never was a Clemons. I was an Aycock and all these years I have been carrying a different last name as to who I really was. My daughter's Dad and I got a divorced after one and a half years of marriage in 1986 and I kept the last name Clemons until 2003. After the second divorce, I was able to go back to my first ex-husband's last name. Through-out the past ten years since the divorce God had been doing a major inner healing in my heart. Through the years He would bring to my remembrance things I had forgotten. I remember a time when God reminded me of the time I had to move back to North Carolina as my Dad or his wife wanted me or my daughter living with them there anymore. I was driving down the highway when I had a vision flashback of that day sitting on my bed at my Dad's house. I was heartbroken that I had to leave him and that I had been lied on. Even having that memory come back still had pain of that day. I was enjoying getting to know my Dad and now I had to leave. I know when God brings back a memory He wants to heal the pain in that area. That was a time in 1987 - it was now 2015. I had buried that so deep that I had forgotten about that day. I asked Jesus to show me where He was during this time and I had saw Him sitting on the bed with me. He was right beside me. He had His arm around me and was comforting me. I then asked Holy Spirit to heal that memory and He did. It doesn't matter where you are or what you are doing, God can and will bring healing in your life, even while driving down a road. God will take you as far back as he needs to in order to heal things. It had been 28 years since that day when God healed that experience. He had been pulling out things that I had buried way deep, so deep I did not even know they were there. Often, I would find myself thinking about my Dad. My heart longed for a relationship with him.

I did not want to go and try to make up for the times he was absent I just wanted to spend time with my Dad and get to know him. I only know his name and birth month and day, but not the year. I really wanted to know him like what kind of food does he like, his favorite color, etc.

It was at that time I knew God had healed my heart over my Dad. I felt no pain as I decided to go back to Aycock that next week. I was actually happy to do so. I thought maybe if my Dad looks for me he will be able to find me under my birth name. I changed my Facebook account along with all my identification to Aycock. God told me why He was telling me I needed to go back to Aycock: going back to my maiden name shows the work God has done in my life and heart.

I hadn't heard or talked to my Dad in so many years that I couldn't keep count. That name, Aycock, his name, that I so wanted and couldn't wait to get rid of because it reminded me of the pain, I was now healed; and, I am able to think about my Dad and carry his last name without any problem. Only God could do that kind of work - not man.

No doctor could have helped me with all that junk in my trunk. Just saying the truth - only God could've helped me. Not only was I to go back to Aycock, I started using my middle name, Jean, which is my Mom's name. I tell you I had it double, my Mom's name and my Dad's last name. Double trouble and double the pain. Psalm 147:3 states He heals the brokenhearted and binds up their wounds. Wow. Just look God holds true to His word. He had bounded up my wounds and healed my broken heart. While their lives are still a mess my life has changed. I no longer carry the pain and hurt of my parents.

I'm telling you for as long as I can remember I have said this verse over and over "for my father and my mother have forsaken me, but the LORD will take me in" Psalms 27:10. With all my heart I can say God had taken this broken woman and did a huge work. He has loved me and nothing I have done changed

His love for me. I wasn't able to see that until my heart was healed of my past pain.

Another thing I've said over my whole life is that God knew what kind of parents I would have so He gave me the absolute best grandparents a person could have.

I believe that God will restore the relationship with my Dad while we are on this earth if he has not already left here. My Dad is on my heart often and I still have a longing to see and talk to him but it's a healthy longing not one out of pain and hurt.

It's kind of like when the Lord told me to go back to my roots I was going back to the name I was born with before all the pain and hurt entered my life. The name I came out of my Mother's womb with when God formed me in her womb. It wasn't until I was ready to let go of the pain that God could heal the pain. It was only once I was healed that I was able to say the name Aycock and that's when I knew that I knew I was healed.

I walked standing tall to the court house to change my last name. I called my Daughter and her Dad and told them I was going back to Aycock. I felt I should explain my reason to the two of them. I know both of them knew how painful it was not having my Dad around. Folks, only God can take a broken shattered pieces of a woman and remove the broken heart and give her (me) a new one. For years and years I walked around with a heart covered by self-made band aids trying to cover the pain and brokenness. Band aids don't heal the wound it just keeps it from getting dirty. He did not remove the band aids and mend the brokenness in my heart He removed the brokenness all together and gave me a new heart. One filled with His love. A godly love not broke love, one that doesn't come with stipulations. God's love is a love no matter what, unconditional. To me a broken love is a conditional love that I love you if ....

In the end, the reason that I am able to work through this is because I have forgiven my Dad for not being in my life. He never did anything to hurt me other than being absent. No matter what, he is my Dad and will always be my Dad. And just like my Mom, if there should come a day when I get a call from him I will go rushing to be by his side and do whatever is needed. It's a different situation from my Mom and the issues surrounding our relationship. My Mom has been verbally abusive towards me and it seems like she tried to break the very best of me. It seemed as if I could never do anything right in her eyes and I worked to be accepted but never quite measured up. My Dad was an absent Dad. No abuse. No brokenness - just absent. I wanted to help my Dad. I pray there will be a day when he needs me. We cannot go back in the past but we can start where we are in the present and move into the future.

Again, had I not chosen to forgive the absence of my Dad it could have caused my heart to be filled with a lot of different negative emotions and I would not be where I am today. I believe because I forgave my Dad, I was able to be healed of the spirit of rejection and the orphan spirit, for in return I was able to accept the love of Jesus. That is the power of walking in forgiveness.

4
Take Me, Let Him Live

It was October 16, 1990, the day my world was rocked. When I came home from work that day Granddaddy was lying on the bed not feeling good. Grandma was outside doing yard work and I stepped into the bedroom to show Granddaddy my new eye glasses that I just got. They were red and now all three of us wore glasses. He told me he liked them and Grandma had left the pinto beans out for me to eat. My Daughter and I were at the kitchen table eating when I heard Grandma through the open bedroom window ask Granddaddy to unplug the leaf blower. He got up to do so when I heard him fall. A sound I had heard many times but this time was different he wouldn't talk to me or move. Grandma came rushing in and I yelled at my Daughter to go next door to get Harold who was an EMT. Harold's whole family were EMT's, all three came rushing within a few minutes of Granddaddy falling. I watched and watched as they pumped his heart. I'm sure Grandma was praying and I was standing there not knowing what to do. My Daughter didn't understand but I knew enough to know this was not good. It was the day I cried out to God, "TAKE ME, LET HIM LIVE!" It was the day that I watched the EMS work on my Granddaddy. Not just my Granddaddy but the only man in my life that I loved who truly loved me. The man who never once hurt me. The man my world wrapped around. The love of my life. That the very one life had just left. God please let him live he is a good man. I thought to myself, take me let me die. My life is nothing, but a mess please take me, let me die, I am nothing, take me from this pain I call life. God please TAKE ME LET HIM LIVE! All the while, my little girl, 5 years of age, is standing right beside me. Her little eyes watching, not understanding what is going on. It's her Grandpa lying on the floor, what is happening here? I don't understand. I told her to hop in the car and off we rushed to the hospital at a high rate of speed. I recall her saying Momma slow down. When she said those words I realized how fast I was going and I slowed down. We got to the hospital before the ambulance and were standing at the dock waiting. Then here comes the red lights flashing the siren loud as loud can be as if saying move out of our way we have an emergency in here. They were rushing to get him into the hospital. His stomach rose so high looking like he was nine months pregnant. His skin really dark not the white skin he was. As we waited, the doctor came in and said the words no person wants to hear "sorry he didn't make it". I'm thinking God, WHY did you take him? WHY? WHY? WHY? You should have taken me! The doctor offered us the chance to go say our goodbyes. Grandma and I took hands and walked down that hall slowly knowing our lives just changed forever. The rest of the family stayed in the waiting room. No one wanted to take that walk to join us. Now I knew he was gone and my lady bug Grandma was alone. Okay, I can do this, I am strong, we will make it through this; I thought to myself as we prepared to go see him. That was the day I told Grandma I will take care of you.

I was not sure of what we were going to see. All I know is that the image of what I had last seen, I did not want to remember him that way for the rest of my life. As we entered the room the Grand-daddy I was looking at was not the one I had seen coming out of that ambulance. The darkness of his skin was gone and he was back to looking like himself just asleep. Not knowing what the future held for us I knew that when I spoke the words Grandma I will take care of you she knew that I meant it. I did not know what we would face but together we could do it. At that very minute my life changed from being a single Mom, to also being a Granddaughter who was now responsible for her Ladybug, a nick name I called Grandma. That day we went from four to three and I went from two to three. It was us three women of course one being a little blonde hair blue eyes five years old. My family left the hospital and headed back to Grandma's but I was still at the hospital. How could it be that they left me! They wouldn't let me drive so I couldn't leave in my car and my family didn't realize I was absent when they left. As God is always on time a friend called me at that very minute and asked what I was doing. I told him what happened and he rushed to come get me. We all went back to Grandma's that is when they realized they had left me at the hospital!

How ironic the next day I was scheduled for oral surgery. Since I was not able to move it I kept my appointment. In my mind I needed the drugs to help me cope with all that was going on.

Two days later I somehow managed to make it through the family visitation. Once I laid my eyes on my love lying in that casket I saw what my Grandma had done! Out of all the jackets Granddaddy had she buried him in his favorite one. I guess it became his favorite because I asked him to wear it one Sunday. Gee, why that one? His favorite one and the one that I would always remember.

It was a Sunday morning just as usual we were all getting ready to leave the house for church when here comes my Granddaddy out the door. I had seen the jacket he had on and asked him why he hadn't worn the one I had picked out. As a young girl that would be important to me that my Granddaddy would wear what I picked out. To be honest I was tired of seeing a jacket on him almost every Sunday, so I picked out a different one for him to wear. Granddaddy turned and went back into the house and changed his jacket to the one I wanted him to wear. Then coming down the long row of steps he made a wrong move with his wooden leg and came rolling down the steps towards me. Thankfully, he did not get hurt and he laughed it off. However, as a young girl I didn't think it was funny. From that day on that jacket was a memory of that fall and I never asked him to wear it again. Yet Grandma felt the need for him to wear it in his final resting place. I believe she just may have forgotten about that "fall" Sunday.

The next day after the visitation night the family cars showed up to get us to drive the one mile to the church. The very church I grew up in. It was Granddaddy's last time in that church. At first the skies were overcast but when they got to the song How Great Thou Art the sun came out and the stain glass windows of the church lite up.

As more songs were sung and people spoke, my mind went back to the memories of my love. I remember hearing, "Tammy, don't swallow a seed or you will have a watermelon growing in your stomach". Time and time again I could always count on being told that those summer days sitting on the big front porch in that same rocking chair. Time and time again my Granddaddy would warn me about those watermelon seeds. I was a little girl with her watermelon, a mouth full of teeth, and watermelon juice running down her chin. Enjoying my Granddaddy. No spoon or fork was needed. Surprisingly Grandma never had a watermelon patch growing in the front yard with all the seeds we spit out.

I also remember for years there was one Lucky Strike cigarette laying on the living room mantel and Granddaddy telling everyone not to mess with that cigarette. He had finally stopped smoking and decided he wanted to keep that one on the mantel. We never asked why - we just obeyed his words. That cigarette stayed in the same place from the time he stopped smoking until 1987 when they moved from

Durham, North Carolina back to Rougemont, North Carolina. I remember the time when Grandma and I had returned inside the house from doing yard work we were looking for Granddaddy and couldn't find him. Grandma finally did find Granddaddy! He was sitting at the top of the steps going up into the attic. He had the biggest grin on his face to show us that even with a wooden leg and a glass eye he was able to climb the steps to the attic. I'm sure once my Grandma got done with him he never did that again. He had already disobeyed Grandma's orders to never climb those steps! Oh, that grin on his face. One I will never forget. It was a grin that said, "I made it but now am I really in trouble." We could hear each step as he slid down each one by one on his butt to get down. I'm sure he never did that again.

My mind returned back to the service that was now over and the men started to roll Granddaddy out as the family followed behind the casket. Of course Grandma followed right behind the love of her life and I was holding the love of my life's hands. The rest of the family followed in behind us. I thought, I wish I could climb in that casket with him. As they rolled, my memories were rolling. It was just a few months back on Mother's Day that Granddaddy yelled "Lois", his wife and my beloved Grandma, "write Tammy a check for $50.00 for Mother's Day. She doesn't have anyone to take care of her so I will". For them to do that was a sacrifice because it was their retirement income and it was not much. I had not asked for it and was caught off guard to hear that. I bought a pair of jeans with the money and a few other things. I kept those jeans for years and years just because of how I got them. It was November 22, 1999, when the jeans were cut off of me by EMS workers after a bad car wreck. Why did I wear those jeans that day? One of the gifts from my Granddaddy is now cut into pieces with blood all over them.

My mind went back to the many times that Granddaddy and I were playing around and I would always feel his leg to see which one was the wooden leg before I hit his leg playing around with him. There were many times I hit the wrong leg and it felt like I broke my hand. Oh, boy the memories were flowing and the tears were flowing with them. I tried to stop the flow of tears but it was not going to happen. I had oral surgery the day before so I was still in pain from that and needed to take the pain pills to relieve some of the pain from surgery. The pain in my mouth could never compare to the pain in my heart but the pills did numb my emotions some. This man who really loved me was now gone. I would never see him again on this earth but I always heard I would see him again in Heaven. I had no doubt where he went. His life was one with Jesus and he had walked the walk and talked the talk, and if someone was on his property and said something about Jesus or cussed, he told them to watch their mouth or get off his property.

He loved my Grandma. They almost made it to 50 years of marriage before he left. I never heard them fight or argue. Of course Granddaddy knew not to mess with Grandma or she just might get the broom after him or a branch off the tree.

As we said our final goodbyes, I just could not believe that this was happening and I couldn't help questioning why God would allow him to leave us. I was hurt and I was very mad. I tried not to show it but I was a boiling pot of water about to boil over. For a year I carried that pain of God taking my Granddaddy. I didn't want to let go of the anger nor did I want to talk to God. Why? Because He did not listen to me and He took my Granddaddy. It was around a year after my Granddaddy died when a person walked into the store I was working and said to me you are blaming God for everything in your life. To be honest at that time, those words went straight to my heart. I knew they were right and I knew my Granddaddy would not be happy with where I was with God. I just did not know how to handle the pain of him being gone. I also knew my Granddaddy would have chosen to go instead of me dying. He would have gladly given his life for me to live. He had an amazing life full of God and lived to almost 70. I was still young with a long life ahead me and a small daughter to raise. I knew something had to change and I knew I had to get back right with God. I also wanted to see my Granddaddy again so I knew I had to get my act together so I could go to heaven when I died so I could see him. He was the only man that had always loved me and the only man who never hurt me. The man who left the face of this earth without knowing the truth about the things that happened to me. I never found the right time to break his heart to tell him his little girl, his Granddaughter, had been through so much.

I had said my whole life and still to this day, at the age of 54, God knew what kind of parents I had so he gave me the best Grandparents. It wasn't until 1991, a year later, when I went through the inner healing (which you will find in the chapter You've Hurt Me.) that I really came to grips with my attitude towards my Granddaddy's death. It was at that time when I really had to repent and ask God to forgive me of how I was acting and the things that I had done. In the end, the truth was had God answered my prayer that day my Daughter would have grown up without a Mom; and, more than likely I would have gone to hell and not heaven. So God loved me enough to say it's not your time, I have plans for you. The fact is, Granddaddy went to be with his first true love, his Lord Jesus Christ. I believe had it been me to leave first Granddaddy would have been heartbroken.

Yes, I miss him 28 years later but I know there is a day that I will see him again.

5.
Her Hands Were Cold

I heard my boss voice come over my cb radio, "613 come in" as I picked up my radio dispatch mic and I said "go ahead". My boss asked, "What is your location?" "I'm on my way to Y. E. Smith". "Call me when you get there," "10-4". As I called my boss I had the thought they needed me to do another run as they often did. I heard my boss on the other end utter the words "they are trying to get in touch with you where your Grandma is. I have someone on the way to you". I said "do I need someone on the way to me"? He replied "I don't know". As I picked up my cell phone I saw that I had missed a call from the nursing home. I thought Grandma had fallen as usual and they were calling to let me know. Once they answered, I was told the doctor wants to talk to you. Okay, I had asked for her medicine to be changed so maybe they were following up on the medicine. I was placed on hold for them to get him. The first thing out of his mouth was "are you alone"? I said "yes", all I remember about that call was I was told "her hands were cold". At that very moment, I dropped to my knees by the fence I was standing at and let out such a loud cry from so deep within that the other bus drivers came running over to me. My ladybug was gone and had gone to be with her first love, Jesus and my Granddaddy. I tell you that cry was one I have never done before. It came from the very bottom of my heart, very deep inside. One that I will never forget and one that I never want to do again.

October 23, 2012, a day that I will never forget was when my Grandma went home to her final resting place. The day I knew that I would never hear the sweet words "I love you" or "Sugar can I fix you something to eat"? My Grandma and I had a special bond straight from the heart from my very young years. My weekends were always spent at my

Grandparents from as far back as I can remember. Friday nights were spent with Grandma and me cutting patterns that needed to be sewed. After cutting the patterns, the 1957 Kenmore sewing machine would run its course stitching the material together. Grandma was always happy while at the machine. It was a gift from her love, my Granddaddy. That machine sits in my house to this day and it still runs just as it did back when Grandma was sitting at it. Saturday was always cleaning the house, doing the yard and having a huge bon fire of leaves in the ditch. After a long day of work, the final work to be done was washing the car. It had to be clean for church on Sundays. On Sundays we went to church then came home for Sunday lunch, pinto beans, potatoes, Grandma's fried chicken legs and her famous homemade biscuits. Sunday afternoon naps were the best. Grandma taught me more things by her lifestyle than by her words.

She lived her life as a Proverbs 31 woman. She took care of her household and my Granddaddy and of course me. Once Granddaddy had gone, she started going around taking care of the sick people in her church. She delivered meals on wheels and spent countless hours just serving in her church and community. Hours and hours were spent with her ears open to hear what I had to say and at the end of the conversation she would always say "I cannot tell you what to do honey". Really there was no need, because just having that listening ear was what I really needed.

Grandma left this earth never having owned a house or a brand new car and she pretty much lived in poverty her whole life. During my lifetime, while she was here, I will say there was never a time her bills were unpaid. God always made a way, maybe not a lot of money was left over but her utilities were always on and her car always had gas. Grandma believed God would take care of her and He did! Six weeks before she joined the love of her life, she needed to be moved from assisted living to a nursing home. God opened a door for her to go into a high class home. One that I never thought she would be able to get into. But God opened that door. I told everyone including her she may not have had much on this earth but she sure was living with rich people as her last home on earth.

I'm so grateful that our relationship never once hit a bump. She loved me with all my faults and not once did she bring up the mistakes I had made over the years. She tried her best to teach me how to make homemade biscuits; however, that is something I never quite got the hang of. She taught me how to sew and how to can veggies. One Saturday when I woke up from a nap she had the house stinking so bad I thought I was going to get sick from the smell. Grandma was making chow-chow and I tell you Grandma never made that stuff again while I was there. I didn't ask her not to she chose not to. Saturday's was also wash day around the house. We spent a few hours washing one load after the other in the old fashioned washing machine. After each load of clothes was done washing we would go outside in the yard to take the clothes out of the washer to put them through the ringer to wring the water out. This was really old fashion! I can still hear Grandma yell, "keep your finger out of the ringer or it'll take them off." I still have all ten fingers.

I remember another time when we were out in the yard I may have been around 11 or so and a couple of her chickens came after me. When I looked up, I saw Grandma running towards the chickens with her broom. The next visit the chickens were gone! I never asked where they were in fear I may have eaten them!

When I was a teenager I had done something and never confessed to her that it was me that had done it. I had taken some money to buy school supplies. As time was moving along and Grandma was getting older, I knew that I needed to make sure I did not leave anything undone. I didn't want any regrets. So I talked to Grandma and confessed what I had done years ago. I asked her to forgive me and I tell you without a blink in her eye she said she did. From that day to the day she left this earth she never mentioned it again.

As time went on Grandma's mind went more into heaven than here on earth. It was really hard to watch the woman that I loved so much forget who I was. She couldn't remember my name but would tell people I belonged to her. Each time I got ready to leave I had to tell her I had to go to work. I would say I have to go to work to buy you chocolate. With a smile on her face the last thing she would say was when will I see you again? I pretty much went to see her every day or every other day. However, for her, she had already lost the concept of time. What was a minute seemed like hours to her. Her falling became a normal thing and every time she fell they had to call 911. It was the rest home's policy to do so. I got a call she had fallen and they were calling the ambulance. I was able to get to the rest home before EMT. I found her lying on a sheet on the floor covered with a blanket and her head on her pillow. I told them she hadn't fallen, rather she is sleeping on the floor which appeared to be a flash back to her childhood years of lying on the floor. Once EMT got there, we got her up and helped her walk around to make sure she was okay and they checked her out to be sure she had not fallen. She was just fine only slipping more back into her childhood.

Every time my phone rang I always held my breath because I didn't know what to expect on the other end of the line. During one of Grandma's ER visits the doctors wanted to do a MRI because she had fallen and hit her head. I refused to let them. Grandma was 90 years old and at that age brain surgery was not going to happen. They would have had to drug Grandma to get her to be still for the MRI and I decided that that was too much for her and her body so we opted not to have the MRI. There have been times I often wondered if she died from a slow brain bleed and we did not know it. I will always believe that I made the right decision for my Grandma. Grandma was admitted overnight to keep an eye on her. I stayed with her. She was in a rage wanting to go home and they had to put a tent like thing over her hospital bed to keep her in the bed. Once up Grandma was walking the halls hugging everyone she came across. Grandma loved people. She was also a very determined woman and she wanted to go home, and it took everything I had to keep her in that hospital room. As a special needs bus driver I was very well trained in restraining a person. As my Grandma held on tight to that hospital room curtain determined she was going home I was determined she was not going out that room. It was a battle and in the end she won. They ended up discharging her.

On another occasion Grandma had fallen again. I was thirty minutes away from the hospital when I got the call. She was taken to the ER by the EMS drivers. It was different this time. The EMS team stayed with Grandma until I could get to the hospital. Instead of being in a multi-patient room with curtains pulled she was in a room all by herself. As we waited I played Southern gospel music on my phone for Grandma and it was very peaceful. Nurses and doctors got word Grandma was back and they each came in to say hi. In the past six months or so it seemed like Grandma was at the ER at least once a week or more. Many of the hospital staff got to know us. But this time it was different, it felt like they were coming in to say their goodbyes to her as if they would not see her again. I also felt it was her last visit to the ER. As I took her back to the assisted living, arrangements were already being made to move her to the nursing home. She had gotten to where she needed more care than just assisted living.

A few days later I went to get Grandma and move her into her new home. I felt such a peace knowing she would be able to have a lap belt in her wheelchair so there would be minimal chance of falling. As she settled into her new place I visited almost every day. She was getting to the point where she was beginning to be bedridden. I knew she would not want to be totally bedridden because through-out her whole life she had asked God to take her home before she could not take care of herself. While growing up I spent many nights lying on the couch listening to the woman that I loved cry out to God in her bedroom for all of us kids. I never told her I heard those prayers (I did leave that unsaid) but I heard them for years and years. I believe it was her prayers that kept me safe all the years and the same prayers brought me back to Jesus when I walked my own way.

One day I called the nursing home to ask them not to bath her until I got there because I had new clothes for her and I wanted to see how to bed bath her. Once there I noticed she had lost a lot of weight and I had seen her use the bathroom while lying in the bed. I knew she did not want to live like that. She was singing as I was learning how to bathe her in bed. I said "Grandma are you singing" and she said "hush Tammy" at the very minute my heart melted as she remembered my name. I just knew that I knew it would not be long. As I was dressing her I said a little prayer "God if you want to take her home you can". I knew that I had to release her because I knew she did not want to live like that. I had to give up my wants to fulfill her wants. That was a really big step for me to do. I knew once she was gone hearing someone say "I love you" wasn't happening for me anymore other than my daughter. After I got her dressed and placed her back in her wheelchair I got ready to leave. I kept looking back at her and saw a piece of hair in her eyes so I went back to move it. Then I looked back again and went back to get a hug. Maybe something inside me knew that would be the last time I would see her alive. I know that she left this earth knowing I loved her and her, me.

It was two days later when I got the radio call "613 come in". I drove a special needs school bus and 613 was my bus number. After getting off the phone and trying to get myself back together I told God, "If you answered all my prayers that fast we would be alright."   Now let me say even if God didn't answer my prayers we would still be alright. It was sort of a joke because within two days she was gone. I had to call my family members starting with my daughter, then my Uncle for him to tell my Aunt. Then the call to my Mom, the one I didn't want to make.

I was Grandma's power of attorney so pretty much everything was on me. My Aunt and I worked together to plan Grandma's service. No one in the family spoke that day but me. I had to tell about the time I came home and someone was sitting on the front porch in an orange and black toboggan and I didn't know who it was and it was Grandma. Yes, to this day I have that toboggan. Everyone always ask how Grandma cooked her green beans and I gave out her secret that day. I talked about the time Grandma wouldn't allow me to roll down the window in the car because she didn't want the wind to blow her wig off and the time she fell in the backyard so hard it knocked her wig off. Then was the famous time when Grandma, who was always loosing things, lost her teeth. We were sitting around eating popcorn and watching a TV show and Grandma got up looking for her teeth. She was tearing everything up on the couch then she turned around and there were her teeth stuck to her gown on her backside. I tell you we never stopped laughing about that one. I made sure that everyone remembered the Proverbs 31 woman she was. How she served her family, her church, the shut-ins and her community. How she had to go to church after getting out of the hospital from a car wreck. She had just left me and was going home and I was also heading home. That KFC chicken must have been really good and filling to her because she fell asleep while driving and had a head on collision within 50 feet of her driveway. She was kept overnight in the hospital and I was right by her side.

We were released on Saturday and Grandma was determined to go to church that Sunday. I agreed because I knew I would not win the battle. I told her she had to wear pants. Her legs were bruised so badly and she agreed. She never believed in wearing pants to church but that day she did. We went to church in pants and a back brace on her back. I remember she cried the whole service just thankful to be alive. I told stories at her service that reflected the true Grandma I knew. I never gave glory to dementia while she was alive nor talked about it at her service. While she was alive I simply said her mind was in heaven and her body is on earth. That disease took the woman I know into a different place; but, she was still my Grandma. I remember the last time I took her out to eat. The wait staff brought her food out before mine. She finished eating before me and was ready to go. She got up from her seat and threw a fit and landed on the floor. She yelled and kicked her feet while lying in the floor. For some people that would have been embarrassing but I just figured that most people would know what was going on. See you cannot argue with a disease. That wasn't my Grandma acting like that but the disease.

After I paid the bill, I said "Grandma, are you ready to go home"? She said "yes", and I helped her off the floor. This was the same woman that pulled my Daughter's tooth when she was around nine years old while I was at work. As it turns out, my Grandma sat my Daughter on the dryer, tied sewing thread to her tooth, and the other to the door knob. Then she shut the door and out came the tooth. Yes, that was my Grandma. The woman who forgave the crazy mistakes I made growing up. She was the woman who still loved me no matter what. My Grandparents didn't show me love through material things or by buying me things. They showed me real love from the heart. They showed me that with a life with God first, you can overcome anything. They taught me that the Word of God is important in one's life and God is faithful to the end.

I am so glad that day I was honest with my Grandma and told her what I had done and asked her to forgive me. I don't know what life would be like if I had to live with the painful act that I did without my Grandma's forgiveness. True forgiveness is when you forgive and never bring it back up just as my Grandma had done. It really is in the sea of forgetfulness.

6.
Let Him Die

In this chapter you will find me talking about my "Dad". This chapter is about my brother's Dad, my Mom's third husband, my step-Dad who I also call Dad. While the world may say justice was never served, God said yes it was in forgiveness.

I was in my bedroom and I heard Mom locking down the trailer. Daddy (my Step-Daddy) was drinking and was on the war path again. It seemed this is what some would call "the norm" at our house.

I believe the fighting started when I was in middle school. There were fights before but as time went on they became more frequent from weekly to almost daily. It seemed like a normal day around our house. The fights started with words first then turned into physical blows. I don't know who laid the first hit because I always hid in my bedroom. I knew what the first one felt like and tried to stay out of sight so I would be out of mind. Mom and Dad kept the house in an uproar while my brother and I watched. Remember this is the norm for our house. This day it was different, because my Mom was locking him out. I had never seen this since the fights were usually in the house. My step-Dad was drunk and had taken off in the dune buggy. Then I heard that noise - the noise of the window breaking. He had rammed his whole arm in the window by the door to unlock the door. Mom was yelling. As I came out of my bedroom I had seen my Dad and his arm was bleeding very badly. Based on the amount of blood flowing, my guess was it wouldn't be too long before he would bleed to death. I yelled, "Let him die!" Not just once but many times. This man had been taking advantage of me for years sexually, physically and fighting with my Mom. "LET HIM DIE!" I did not want him to live anymore.

He had hurt me enough. No, my Mom did not listen to me. She rushed him to the hospital and he lived.

As it turns out, he had gotten the dune buggy bumper stuck on a rock and couldn't get it off the rock so he had walked back home. Mom told me someone must have put something in his drink while they were at the bar that night. I'm not sure if I believe that because he was always a violent man when drinking. Gee Mom, why could you not let him die when he cut his arm then he would be out of our lives.

Sometime later I had just gotten my driver's license and my Mom let me use her car to go somewhere. As I was pulling up to the house my Mom was standing outside and she yelled that he is on a rage again and she hopped in the car. I drove off and he followed us in that big blue Ford truck. The faster I drove, the faster he drove and he stayed on my bumper hitting the back of the car. I was yelling and my Mom was trying to keep me calm. I had just learned how to drive and this man was pushing us and slamming in the back of the car trying to run us off the road!

Somehow, (God) I was able to get away from him and he stopped.

Dad wasn't always a "bad" man. He seemed pretty decent when he first met my Mom. I was a little girl who did not have a dad in my life and he filled that spot. I remember one time I was walking home when I was around eight years of age and there were some teenage boys following me. I looked up the street and there was my Dad with the tire chains in his hands. He had been working on the car outside and had seen what was going on so he came to help me. He didn't have to say anything to the boys following me because they had seen him and they ran away.

One night Mom and Dad had left my brother and me with his sister while they went out. My Aunt had invited her boyfriend over and something snapped in his mind. He had a fake $100.00 bill (like I didn't know it was fake) and was offering it to me so he could take advantage of me. I was nine years old at the time. As I was running around the table to get away from him he had stepped in some dog poop and fell to the floor. Just as he had fallen my Dad and Mom came in the door to pick up my brother and me. Just in time my rescuers had come I thought. Mom did not press charges on him and she would not allow me to testify against him. My Mom did not want me to testify for some reason so charges could not be filed against him. To this day I remember his name and I will never forget that name nor him chasing me around that house. I never heard anything else about him after that but I am sure he was glad he was never charged

The older I got, the more I got Dad's attention and he started doing things to me. He always told me not to tell my Mom. Everything in me turned when he would come in my bedroom to wake me up by feeling on me. I believe that I was in my early teens when Dad started messing with me.

Then there were times he took me to their bed. It was bad enough he was now penetrating my body but now I was being forced to be on my Mom and his bed while my Mom was away. I remember the bed stinking from having the smell of my Dad. He worked on cars and it smelled like oil and things from a car. Because of the fear of being hurt I laid there and let him do what he needed to do. Yet it was the only attention I ever got so sometimes I felt important. So many thoughts, so much going on in my teenage mind and not being sure what to do. I couldn't tell anyone. I might get killed and I surely could not tell Mom because she wouldn't believe me anyway and I knew I would be a dead girl if I did. I had no doubt that he would hurt me if I told.

I remember the times Mom said she was going to pick me up from school and then sent him. I remember standing outside that high school building seeing the big blue truck pull up. I felt like I wanted to run because I knew what was going to happen. There was a small dirt road and that is where he always pulled off the road before reaching home. I couldn't understand why Mom would send him to pick me up and not come herself. Dad worked Monday through Friday so why was he not at work? Why was I even getting picked up instead of riding the school bus?

For me the school bus was a safe ride home. I really believe my Mom did not know what was going on to start with. As time went on I think she may have known something was going on but did not want to believe it. So many times I felt unclean as a teenager. There were so many times I spent under the trailer crying and talking to God - asking why? Was this really love? He was my Dad so he should love me right? Step Dad or real Dad I felt any Dad should love their child. Maybe he really didn't love me and that is why he would always introduce me as "his step daughter". I don't recall one time when he said this is "my daughter". Maybe in his mind he could not face the pain of what he was doing and calling me "his daughter" would cause deeper pain than just "my step daughter".

So many men, including, my Dad's best friend, his brother, his sister's boyfriend and another babysitter's husband. What was it that these men wanted from this very young girl?

Then there was the man at the candy store pulling me into the back room when I went to get candy when I was about eight years old. I don't remember anything other than the candy store man taking me into another room. I just don't remember.

About the same age, eight or nine years old, Mom and Dad would take my brother and me to another babysitter while they went out dancing. I remember the babysitter's husband grabbing my personal area inside my pants. I was so young, yet I knew what he was doing was wrong but did not know what to do about it. Then there was an incident where my Dad's brother started touching me in places. He had called me over to him while he lay on the bed in a full body cast from being shot. I thought he wanted some water or something and then he reached out his hand and grab my private areas. I may have been around nine or 10 then. Then the true hurt came when my step-Dad started doing the same thing all the other men were doing to me. I was crushed.

A few years later the guy that ran the Moose Lodge where my family and I would often go, started asking me if I wanted to come clean the Moose Lodge to make some money. So like every other high school teenager, who wanted to have money of their own, I took him up on his offer. By no means did I know what I was in store for. Things were going well and then here we go again. This man who was triple my age started coming towards me. It wasn't for sex this time. What he wanted was for me to pose in lingerie. He started buying it and as time went on he started taking pictures. Then came a time when he wanted a girlfriend of mine to come with me. My friend Cindy started going to the Moose Lodge with me and together we posed in lingerie for him to take pictures. I kept going to the Moose Lodge for a few months to clean.

Everyone thought I was cleaning but the truth was I was posing for pictures. Then came the day he wanted pictures with no clothes on so there I was. I was posing in front of the man with no clothes while he took pictures. I don't recall how it stopped but I believe that it was because I decided I was not going back to The Moose Lodge. It may have even been when I was old enough to get my driver license and a car so I could work a real job.

Growing up, I never understood and to this day I still don't know what it was about me that caused men to want to touch my little body as a child? My Dad waited until my teenage years to start his mess but for the men before, it did not matter that I was so young. I did not like what was going on but at some point in time I started to believe that this is what life should be like for me. I may have even gotten use to the touches and the penetrations. Maybe that is how man expressed love by; touching and feeling a little girl. Could it be? I didn't know.

When the time came for my monthly, I had missed my period at 16 years of age and I had to tell Mom that I didn't have my period and tell her what Dad was doing to me. I did not know what she was going to do but I had to tell her. I knew that I was taking a chance of really getting hurt by my Dad but I needed to do this. I had gotten use to his belt on any area of my body when I had done something so it was no big deal. Another beating wouldn't kill me. I had to find my voice and tell my Mom. Things did not go as I planned and before I knew it I was packing my bags and moving into my Grandparents home. My Mom was hurt and mad and at first she did not want to believe what I told her. Things were hard in the house after I told her and she called my Grandma to see if I could move in with them. Of course my Grandparents said yes. In her mind it was my fault all this happened.

I told my Grandma but my Granddaddy never knew even the day he died he was never told. It would have broken his heart beyond repair. Then once I was settled in at Grandma's, my Mom stopped talking to Grandma. I could see the pain of her daughter not talking to her weighing on her shoulders. So I had a choice, to move back home or to stay with Grandma and be the reason Mom would be not talk to her. Because My Grandma did not know the full story of what had happened to me, she thought that it only happened one time with my Dad. I did not tell her about the other men. I knew my Grandma loved me very deeply and I knew if I told her everything it would also crush her heart. I loved my Grandma very much and wanted to protect her heart. I went back home to save my Grandma's heart and to try to bring peace between my Mom and her. My Grandma did not stop talking to my Mom. My Mom was the one to cut off all communications with Grandma. However things went back to normal when I moved back home. So I stayed with Mom during the week and on the weekends I spent with my Grandparents.

Once I was back with my Mom and Dad, he never touched me again! My car broke down again and my Mom called one of my Dad's friends who worked on cars. Roger told my Mom to tell me to bring the car over to him and he would look at it. My Dad also worked on cars but one of the ways of taking advantage of me was he would fix my car but I would have to pay by sleeping with him. He wasn't touching me anymore so him fixing my car was over. I left the house to go to Rogers and had packed an overnight bag to spend the night with my Grandparents who lived right down the road from Roger and his wife. Once I got to Roger's house I pulled into the driveway and he met me outside. I asked where his wife was and discovered she was not at home. It was at that time he took my hand and pulled me in the house. I did not want to go because I knew what was going to happen. Roger had never made a move on me before and I never thought he would. But here I was again in the same place that I had been many times before. I did not like nor want what happened in the house and I was crushed. I cared about this man and his wife and considered them to be a part of the very few people I trusted. I was in distress with nowhere to turn and nowhere to run. He was a very big man, more than triple my size and very strong. I could not get away. After he was done, I walked out the door and got in my car without it being fixed. I had to get myself together to call Grandma to tell her I had changed my mind about spending the night and was going to stay home. I had to drive by her house on the way home from leaving Roger's and it broke my heart to see that house. To know the people there loved me so much but yet I chose not to tell them what was going on. I just couldn't, I did not want to break their heart. I had made a promise that if another man touched me in an unwanted fashion I would kill them! Thankfully I never had to kill anyone! I really believed at that time in my life if a man had touched me I would have done everything I could to kill him. It did not matter who it was I could have committed murder. I was over the men taking advantage of me and I was old enough now to do something about it.

Once my Daughter was born I made sure that I never left her alone with my Dad. Never! It was 1991 when God started doing the inner healing in me and I knew that I had to forgive this man. God had been impressing on my heart that I had to forgive people so I could move on with my life. I needed to be healed and wasn't able to until I forgave. So I did forgive him as God worked on the inside of me. I forgave him but I still would never leave my Daughter alone with him. I got a call in 1993 that he had fallen off a roof and had broken his back. My brother and I moved into his home to help take care of him. It was only by the grace of God that the pain was out of me and I had forgiven him and was able to help him. Daddy never mentioned it to me to this day and has never asked me to forgive him. Forgiveness is not about the other person, the one who did the hurting; it is always about the one who was hurt that needs to forgive. You see forgiving him sets me free from the pain and hurt. I don't know if he has ever forgiven himself or not. I still see him from time to time and I still call him Daddy. He and Mom divorced in 1987 a year after my divorce so the truth is he is no longer my "step" Dad. However, to me he will always be my Dad. Not my "real" Dad but the only "father figure" in my life for any length of time during my early years.

Forgiveness is the key to healing. Matthew 6:14-15. "For if you forgive other people when they sin against you, your heavenly Father will also forgive you. But if you do not forgive others their sins, your Father will not forgive your sins." I felt if I did not forgive those men that had done these things to me I would not be forgiven of the things I had also done in my life. If

Dad should need me again I would be there to help because the past is in the past. Both of us may leave the face of this earth never talking about what happened. I may never know if he is sorry for what he did. As for me, I don't need to know that to move on. God has done the work that no man can do and that is the power of walking in forgiveness. I am thankful that Mom did rush my Dad to the hospital that day and did not listen to me. I was speaking and acting out of pain and hurt. If my Mom had listened to me, my brother would have grown up without his Dad. I pray that there will be a day coming when my brother is also able to forgive his Dad and be able to move on with his life. My Brother has never dealt with the pain of his Dad and the things that happened around the house. While a lot of the things that happened in our household were not directed towards my brother he still witnessed it.

I'm not sure, had my Dad died that day he cut his arm forgiveness would have taken place as it did later in my life. Why would it be necessary if the person is dead? Do you really need to forgive someone who is dead? I believe so because as I mentioned earlier it's not about the other person but it's about you, the one who needs to forgive.

I had gone several years without seeing my Dad then came the day my Mom moved into the same boarding house that my brother lived in. Often when I went to get my Mom's clothes or take her groceries and things my Dad was there. Amazing and only because God had healed me from the past pains and hurts of this man that I now can look at him face to face. I was able to remember the past but not the pain. See God calls us to forgive not forget. While this area in my life may be the hardest road I only made it through because I chose to forgive the man that I called Dad. I no longer have fear when I see him thinking that it will happen again. I leave the past in the past. That is not how the world see's justice. To them justice was not served for what he did. God's justices said forgive! I don't know what he deals with on the inside knowing what He did to me, but what I know is this. Forgiveness is the biggest justice that can be served and that only comes through God.

7.
You're Pregnant

Many people may not agree with me but I stand firm that when I was told I was pregnant for me it was a miracle from God. It was at a time in my life when I was drinking and doing drugs heavily. I loved staying high so I did not have to deal with the things that had happened and were still going on in my life. I knew from the moment I found out, I said to myself that I would not be a Mom like my Mom. I stopped smoking, drinking and doing drugs immediately. It was all for the baby I was carrying. I was over joyed that I was going to have a baby even though I was 19 years old. I was going to have someone to love and who would love me in return. To be honest that baby growing inside of me is the very reason I lived.

The hardest thing was to tell my very Christian Grandparents that I was pregnant and not married. Sex outside of marriage was a sin in their eyes. I am sure I rehearsed in my head how I was going to break the news to them.

A few days later I went to my Mom's and there was my Daughter's Dad outside with everyone. He had a folding chair in the yard and a circle drew in the dirt. He sat me down and then got on one knee and asked me to marry him. I said yes. A few months later we got married. I borrowed my Aunt's wedding dress and her veil thankfully the veil covered the half zipped dress. It was a small wedding and the person that made the cake for us made it blue, pink and yellow. Baby colors so everyone would know there was a baby on the way. My Grandparents were at the wedding. They truly loved me and they were not happy I got pregnant while unmarried. But, their love for me out weighted what I had done. They were excited to become great grandparents. Plus they loved my daughter's Dad!

Moving along in the pregnancy I stayed sick day and night. I had to keep crackers beside me at all times. I was gaining weight like crazy especially since I had stopped smoking and doing drugs. The more weight I gained the more my back hurt. I ended up being on bed rest almost the whole time I was pregnant. My baby was moving more and more and kicking a lot. I was excited that I was finally going to have someone to love me and for me to love as well.

Before I got pregnant I was not at a good place in my life. I really wanted to check out of this world and had thought about it many times but just couldn't. First of all, I don't like pain and I knew if I took my life it was going to hurt even if only for a few minutes. I knew I didn't like pain and here I was pregnant! In my heart, I knew that even though God does not cause us to sin nor does He have any part of sin - I knew that He had allowed me to get pregnant and it really did save my life.

It was 1984 and they said Michael Jackson won entertainer of the year. As soon as it was announced, some of my water broke through. I got out of the bed, took a shower, changed the sheets on the bed and called Mom. Off to the hospital we went. The next day I had a beautiful little girl that hurt me so bad coming into this world. It was a long labor and a dry birth and a back that could not stand the pressure or pain. The epidural did not work; I felt everything and even more.

I didn't have a good example of how to raise a child so as time went by I made many mistakes. I was doing the best that I could do with what I knew to do. It really upsets me when people say that when someone has been abused they usually also abuse. That is the farthest thing from being true with me. I made a point to be a lot better Mom than my Mom.

As my Daughter grew up - I grew up. We grew up together. I was so proud of my little girl. I took lots of pictures and I've kept everything from happy meal boxes to her first sucker. I didn't have those things from my childhood so I wanted to make sure I kept everything and journal a lot about how she was growing up. When my daughter was 15 months old I became a single parent. I didn't know what love was and couldn't accept his love. I was too young and too broken on the inside to be married. I knew he really loved me and I loved him the best I could. In the brokenness, I realized that I did not know how to accept love or give love. I had no clue what love was other than in the bed and that wasn't love at all, it was just sex. Let me say that my Daughter has an amazing Dad; it was the brokenness in me that did not want to stay in the marriage. He was a good husband to me and a good Dad. I was the one who could not accept his love. Just as I always did I had a wall up and ran from things so I wouldn't get hurt. My past proved to me that when I love something it hurts me so I left before he had a chance to hurt me. Had I not left we probably would still be together to this day.

When she was three years old we were back in church and I gave her to God. I told God if she was going to die and go to hell, I wanted him to take her before she knew the difference between right and wrong. As my one and only was growing up I lived in a lot of fear that someone might abuse her the way that I had been abused. I was very protective and never left her with a male friend. If a male friend and I were going somewhere and she was with us I made a point to always keep her in my eye sight without anyone knowing. Fear gripped me so hard and so deep. Often I would ask her has anyone touched you anywhere on your body. I never explained to her why I was asking and tried to ask in a way that she wouldn't figure out why I was asking. I never wanted to put fear in her. Later in her teenager years I told her why I would always ask the questions. Before then I was so careful how I asked she never knew and was able to live a life without fear.

As she grew into a teenager, then a young woman I knew if anyone made an unwanted move on her she would be able to protect herself. I was able to let go of that fear that once bound me and enjoy the woman she was becoming.

Even though my Daughter and I were always close, those teenage years did provide some trying times. The fact that she was a teenager and that she had attitudes from her Dad and I in her definitely proved to challenge our relationship at times. Many times I could see myself in my daughter and then there were times I could see her Dad. She was becoming a strong independent young woman much like her Mom. I believe she was a little head strong and she got that from both of us even though I joke and say it came from her Dad.

I worked very hard to give her a different life than I had and I guess you can say I worked too hard to do so. There were times when we had our differences for sure but for the most part we were like sisters instead of mother and Daughter. I really did grow up the same time she was growing up. Our relationship was and is a very close one. I made a lot of mistakes raising my one and only but the good thing is she never held it against me. Even during the times when it was the hardest. Like when we were homeless and I had to send her to her Dad's because I was not able to take care of her. It broke my heart to do so but I was sick and dying and was not able to take care of myself.

Just in time God bought a friend back into my life, who I had not seen in a couple of years and together (more him than me) my daughter was able to come back to live with me. He helped me take care of her and at the same time he also took care of me.

I watched as my Daughter as she grew up, graduated from high school and then off to college and moving out. I was so proud of the woman she had become. God took all the ashes of my childhood, added in all my mistakes and my heart's desire to me a good Mom and he gave me one amazing daughter. Even with all she went through with my mistakes God made sure she did not have a broken spirit or low self-esteem. God made something beautiful in my Daughter from my ashes.

Over the years, and time and time again, I would always say "I LOVE YOU"! I would say to her, you are amazing; you can do anything you set your mind to do. I always encouraged her. Even in my own brokenness I was able to move past that or more like bury it down deep to raise my Daughter.

We did without a lot of things in the years I was a single parent, (by choice) but the one thing we did not go without was love. We loved each other. She truly loved me and I her to the best of what I knew love to be. Love wasn't about material things; had it been there it would not have been love in our home. To me, love was about spending time together and doing things together. Love was looking at each other and being able to say "I'm sorry, I was wrong". Love was real love with my Daughter not a soul tie from brokenness. It was real. A love that said I will do anything for you. As my Daughter grew I was learning about love and how to love.

Here's the thing, early on in my Daughter's life I had not been healed of my brokenness from the past. I really didn't know what love was. But then I realized that God knew that when he formed my Daughter in my womb. He knew I didn't know what love was. Love hurts was how I defined love. He knew I didn't know how to give love because it's hard to give something when you don't even know what it is. He also knew that I couldn't receive love because I had walls all around my heart. But God knew all that and yet He was still able to show me through my Daughter what love was and how to love. He showed me that real love was unconditional. Only God could have placed that love in me for my Daughter. He knew without Him it was impossible.

She's 34 now and one amazing woman. I don't know how other than to say "BUT GOD" that I raised a girl who became an awesome woman. She still has her Dad and me in her as I see it. But more than anything she is her own person. I am so blessed to be able to call her my Daughter and I'm thankful for who God made her to be. It wasn't me or she would have been like me, a mess! It was all God. Only He can take ashes and turn them into beauty.

There have been times when I've had to ask my Daughter to forgive me but more so I've had to ask God to forgive me. Our relationship truly has not been a bed of roses and it has had many thorns. I can say this, the thorns were removed through forgiveness and once forgiven we've been able to move on.

8.
Burnt Hands

It was September 8, 1972 when I became an older sister. I was no longer the only child. I had a little brother. My brother got really sick right after he was born. He had yellow jaundice and almost died. He was in the hospital for a while. I remember how protective Mom was over him as any Mom would be when their baby is sick. My brother started growing and started walking. We had moved into another house and this house had a grill like thing in the floor for the heat to come into the house. (Sorry I don't know what it is called.) He still wasn't walking very well and he took a fall landing on that grill thing. It was winter time and when he fell his hands landed on the grill. It was so hot he got third degree burns on his hands. I remember Mom standing outside with it being really cold waiting to go to the ER. I don't recall if Dad came or if it was an ambulance. When they got home he had both hands wrapped up so much they looked like a ball. Mom also had to put him back on the bottle because he crushed his front teeth. His hands healed but left both hands with a grill mark on them.

My brother and I have never been really close mainly because of the age difference between us. Each year seems to draw us further apart than the year before. We are also on different paths. He is on the same path I was on in my younger years and the same one as our Mom. My brother's words to me were, "I don't know how you move on." Forgiveness gives a person the ability to be able to move on. Without forgiveness you never are able to move on and are stuck in the same spot for years and years. It was only forgiveness that allowed me to put the past in the past and to move on with my life.

I miss my brother and would love to have a relationship with him. It's sad to see how carrying pain and hurt and unforgiveness can destroy lives. I see it every day with my brother and Mom. I keep praying!

9.
I Didn't Know

In this chapter I will talk about my decision to have an abortion in 1987. I was 23 years old and honestly I did not understand the procedure of having an abortion. At the time I was only around four weeks into the pregnancy and not knowing the truth, I went through with the abortion. Never had I even thought that it was a baby.

Allow me to set the stage for this chapter. When I was pregnant with my daughter I was placed on complete bed rest for most of the pregnancy. I inherited a lower back disorder when I was born which caused severe lower back pain. Carrying the extra weight of the baby put a lot more stress on my back. I also stayed sick the whole term while carrying my baby girl. Birthing was more than I could bear with my lower back and complications of a "dry" birth. I knew the day that my daughter was born I did not want to carry another child or birth one.

When having relationships with a man precautions were taking along with me having an IUD. I wasn't sleeping around taking a chance that I would or would not get pregnant.

The summer of 1987 it was a weekend my daughter would go to her Dad's so Mom and I went to our usual night life spot, TT's bar. She often sat at the bar and had a few beers and I played pool. I noticed there was a new guy there and he rocked this girl's eye! He had come in from Atlantic Beach and was staying in Durham, NC for work. We talked a lot and that conversation moved us into dating. As time went by when he was in town he would stay with me at my Mom when my Daughter was at her Dad's house for the weekend. We got along great and often had adult fun together. I wasn't worried about getting pregnant because I had the IUD.

Then that one day when I was really hungry and there was no food in the house for me to eat, what I would consider to be food. Times were hard because neither my Mom nor I were working. I didn't have transportation to get back and forth and was looking for employment near where we had just moved to. After checking further, I found a can of spinach in the cabinet and I started heating it up. Now I know that I don't like cooked spinach but when you are hungry you will eat just about anything, I believe. Once I opened the can and it started to heat up it had a smell and off to the bathroom I went. That smell made me sick! I decided to go hungry and could not eat that spinach.

A few days later I knew that I knew something was wrong. How could it be that I was pregnant? I had an IUD so I couldn't get pregnant. That's what it is for, so you don't get pregnant! Then I remembered the time I fell at work in the cooler a few months back and broke my tailbone. I had gone to the doctor to get checked and I even got the doctor to check the IUD just to make sure that my fall had not done any harm to me and it was still in place. The doctor told me everything was good and it was still in place. How could it be that a few months later the smell of the spinach was making me sick? I knew that I knew I was pregnant. I had been down this road before and I knew. I did the test using pee and it was negative. Still knowing I went to get a blood test done just to see what the results were. I got the results and it was what I already knew, postive. The doctor found the IUD had moved just a small amount which allowed me to get pregnant. They also removed the IUD that same day. My heart almost stopped! What was I going to do? I'm raising one child and cannot afford another one. There is no way that I can be out of work until the baby is born. I knew with my back and carrying a child I would be placed on bed rest again like I was with my Daughter. The truth is my back was not strong enough to carry a child. It's not like I didn't take precautions to avoid getting pregnant. I did take precautions. I had the IUD and even after the fall I was responsible enough to make sure they checked it. Regardless, it was a fact. There was no way I could change it; I was pregnant.

I really felt like I didn't have a choice but to have an abortion. I made the appointment and told everyone that when the doctors found the IUD in the wrong position and had to remove it which they really did, it caused me to miscarry. I really did not miscarry. I was protecting myself from what people would say or think about me. Folks now I know that what I did was wrong. At that time I was in a really bad place. I had not gone through all the inner healing and was still carrying a lot of hurt and the pain of rejection from my childhood. There was so much junk in my trunk and I kept putting more and more stuff in it. The junk in my life was overflowing out. I felt alone in this situation especially by not telling anyone the truth not even the Dad. I was afraid and embarrassed and not wanting the shame that goes along with it.

I did not have transportation; so, my Mom got her friends to come over in their RV. They took me to the hospital clinic to have the procedure done. I walked down the hall to that office room alone. There were a lot of feelings going through my mind yet still believing I had to do what I was doing. I don't recall if the doctor's talked to me about other options or not. I'm guessing not because I was set in my mind that this was what I had to do. I had to be able to work and could not be on bed rest. After the birth of my daughter I was sure I could go through that again. In my mind this was the only choice for me. My Mom and her friends stayed in the RV until I called them to be picked up. Afterwards, they came to the front to get me and we went home. Looking back even to this day, I walked out of that office without any shame or anything. I knew that it was something I had to do. A few months later I told the guy I was dating and he told me "you took my only chance of being a Dad". I didn't think about that when I made the decision to have the abortion. All I thought about was what my past pregnancy was like. Being in the bed the whole time, staying sick and the pain of having her. David and I continued to see each other for a short time afterwards. His job ended in Durham and he went back to Atlantic Beach. I drove down once to see him but things were never the same between us.

In 1997, I decided that I wanted to start dating again. It had been a long time since I had been in a relationship. I had male friends I hung out with but was longing for a boyfriend. The first thing I did was make a phone call to a women's clinic. I knew what I had to do first; I was not taking any more chances. I made an appointment to have my tubes tied and BURNT! Once in the doctor's office my doctor told me I don't want to do the procedure you are too young and may change your mind. I was 33 years old. I told the doctor I would never change my mind and explained to him my past. He agreed to do the procedure after I told him I wanted to date again and if I got pregnant it would be murder and suicide at the same time. I wasn't planning on having sex but I also know things happen and I wanted to make sure I was never in the same position I was before.

I had turned back to serving God and He was doing a lot of inner healing in my heart. It started with forgiveness and this time it was that I had to forgive myself! I had to forgive myself for having the abortion.

This was also during that time when I started learning about abortions and what they really were. I realized that when I had the abortion, I really didn't know what they were. I didn't know that it was a real baby with a real heartbeat. I honestly didn't think at that time the egg and sperm had been there long enough to form a baby. I just didn't know the truth things may have been different. I will say this; I know a lot of people who have openly admitted in the later part of their life that they had an abortion. I know a lot of people who to this day, years and years later, still carry the pain and shame of having an abortion. For me and for me alone I have never carried pain or shame or regret over having the abortion. I guess it's because once I found out the truth I asked God to forgive me and I know He did. How can you carry shame for something when you walk in God's forgiveness of that thing? I just don't believe that way. I don't live in regret because I believe that is a trick from the enemy - trying to put you in bondage. I look at it this way. At that time I did not know what an abortion really was so to me at that time it was not murder. I did not know it really was a baby already formed (I was only around 4 weeks). I will not allow the enemy to put shame on me for something I did not know and also something that I have asked to be forgiven for and know that God forgave me. Nowhere will you find God saying you are forgiven but you need to carry the pain of what you did. Forgiveness is just that forgiveness. Once you ask for forgiveness you are forgiven. So many times you find women still carrying the pain of an abortion because they are unable to forgive them self for what they have done. That's self-shame that you are putting on yourself and you are allowing the enemy to keep you in bondage over that and you are not able to walk in full forgiveness or freedom.

There are times when I wonder what my second child would be like. They are good thoughts not anything that would create in me a spirit of brokenness, shame or guilt. I know that one day I will meet my child when I get to heaven. Boy or girl - I don't know. Name I don't know. I do know once I get to heaven my child will know who I am there and we will meet. Until then, I live my life in forgiveness and in the fullness of who Jesus is and what His Word said. I am forgiven. Again, I will say I don't live in regret and I don't regret what I did. Thank God for His forgiveness! Why do I keep repeating myself about shame? Because there are people who will read this book and try to put shame on me.

10.
He Never Left Me

Hebrews 13:5, "Let your conduct be without covetousness: be content with such things as you have. For He Himself has said, "I will never leave you nor forsake you."

As a child I would go to church with my Grandparents' almost every Sunday. Back in those days they lived a good ways from church so they only went on Sunday morning, being that they had a very tight budget and gas for a car could blow the budget. Then once I got to around 10 years old or so I would ride the church bus to a local church that I ended up growing up in alone (I was the only one from my family that went there). My Mom and Dad (step) did not go to church. I'm thankful for Christian Grandparents that took me to church with them and raised me with a Christian background. I had heard my whole life Jesus would never leave me. Never means NEVER. Growing up and even as a young adult I did not realize the importance of NEVER.

So many times as a young adult and a young single Mother I tried to get things together. I went to church, taught Sunday school, and loved the people at church. At that time in my life I had a lot of pain from my childhood that I buried down deep so I was in and out of church a lot. It's like I would go then give up and go back into the world. When I was in the world I did things that I knew was not pleasing to God. I went to bars, got drunk, had sex, did drugs and lived my life how I wanted to live it. I thought about God a lot and knew that I was living wrong. I wanted to change and I really wanted to do right in his eyes but yet I just could not get it together. I didn't know why things just did not work for me.

I knew enough and heard that no matter what Jesus would never leave me even in the dark times when I was doing things I shouldn't be doing. I never had the guts to tell God to leave me alone or that I didn't want Him with me. I felt like if I did He would never come back. So I lived my life the way I wanted in the times I was out of church. I didn't talk to God or think much about Him in those days. But the one thing I knew, He was with me all the time even if I was not with Him. I often would think, God if you will never leave me then why did all that stuff happen to me? Why were the men able to do the things to me that they did? I guess in a way I thought God didn't love me and that is why things turned out the way they did in my life.

In 1991, a few weeks after the stranger walked into the store and told me that I was blaming God for everything that happened in my life. Shortly after I heard a song on the radio, "He Never Left Me". It hit me so hard that I had to go buy the cassette. I listened to that song over and over. I knew that

God loved me and no matter what I was doing He would not leave me. I didn't try to take advantage of it I just didn't really know how to love and accept His love while I had all that junk inside of me. It was hard to receive His love when I didn't know what love was.

The lyrics to the song is
Chorus:
He never left me, though I turned my back on Him
Living in a world of sin, trying to run away again.
He never left me, when I chose to walk away.
Even when I couldn't pray, He never left me.

Verse
So many directions, the roads look the same
He gave me instructions, I disregarded in shame
Then sudden destruction soon came my way.
I'll have to say, I've got me to blame.

Verse
I chose a wrong road because it looked good to me
I walked blindly onward, I just could not see

I was lost and I was dying, but now I am trying

I reached out to Jesus; you know He reached out to me.

I felt like God was telling me to write letters to everyone that hurt me. As I listened to that song and laid on my bed and wrote letters, I poured out my heart on that paper covered in tear drops. Yes, God was healing me but more importantly I was realizing that God truly loved me and had never left me even in my darkest hours.

Then I asked God if you never left me where were you when all that happened with the men? He explained to me, see I (God) cannot change man's free will but I (God) can change their heart. Every person has a free will and knows the difference between right and wrong. Those men knew what they were doing was wrong but they were acting in their free will even though it was against my (God's) will. Wow! I thought all these years, "You didn't love me because you allowed that to happen." I knew then that God couldn't stop it because it was done out of their free will. Then I asked, "Okay then, where were you?" His response was, "I was holding your hand". My heart broke. He was holding my hand as that happened. See all I was focused on was what was going on around me that I couldn't even feel God with me. I was so broken over what I had just learned and I was very sorry that I had put the blame on God for something that He could not control but yet He stayed with me while it happened.

A few years went by and I was half and half with the Lord once again. At this time I knew Jesus but still did not have a relationship with Him. I had tried again and it seemed that I just couldn't get it right. I had met this guy Bill at a Christian campground. He was a pastor and away from God due to a divorce. When his wife left him he left turned his back on God. We started seeing each other. Shortly afterwards, I went to his house for us to go riding on his Harley Davidson. Somehow we ended up in the bedroom. Once we finished making out, I looked to the corner of the room and saw Jesus sitting in a chair with His hands over His eyes. In the natural Jesus wasn't sitting there but it was a vision I had just seen. I was heartbroken that I had done something that caused Jesus to close His eyes. I told Bill about it and that was the last of my having sex. That's when God started speaking to me about the Scripture He will never leave you nor forsake you. See there are a lot of things we do in our lives that are not fit for Jesus to see or hear. Honestly, I didn't get this to the extent that I do now until that vision. Because Jesus cannot lie and He said in His word that He would never leave us nor forsake us He goes where we go. He sees what we see. He lives inside of us when we accept Him into our life. Since Jesus knows no sin and cannot be in sin He cannot see or hear the things we are doing and the places we take Him.

Therefore, He couldn't stay in the kitchen when I went into the bedroom I took Him with me into that bedroom. Not His choice but mine. He couldn't leave me because then He would be a liar and He's not a liar. He couldn't watch what I was doing because it was sin. God showed me a vision of Jesus covering His eyes because He could not look what I was doing. Just like watching a movie or TV there things that he shouldn't be watching and covers His eyes. When we are in conversations we shouldn't hear, He is putting His fingers in His ears so He doesn't hear it. You know the truth is I never really thought a lot of what I was doing in that area until that one day. That forever changed my life as to what I watch, places I go and things I listen to.

Now, I try to live my life so that Jesus doesn't have to cover His eyes or put his fingers in His ears. All that time I was doing what I wanted to do and taking Him places I shouldn't, He never left me.

Many times I am sure that had He not been with me, I would have gotten killed. I've been shot at several times and had He not been there I just may have died because that bullet would have hit me. The times I was so drunk and went off with people

I had no clue who they were - He was right with me. He never left me. Many times I remember saying Jesus if you let me live, when I was riding with someone very drunk and speeding down the highway, I will live for you. Again, He never left me. I am thankful that His word is true and He always does what He says. He never left me. Because of His love for me and His patience with me and teaching me, I now understand He will never leave me nor forsake me. And because of His love for me I now understand and respect that my eyes are His eyes, my ears are His ears and I try to live my life according to how and what He would do, see and say. No, I'm not perfect but He knows that and still loves me and understands me because He lives in me.

11.

You've Hurt Me

That day in 1991 was use like any other day. I was a twenty-nine years old single Mom working at a BP gas station trying to make that dollar to pay the bills and raise my seven year old Daughter. Life was difficult for me at that time. I woke up in the morning around 7 a.m. Got my daughter off to school, went to work, got off, picked my Daughter up, cooked dinner, then it was time to get her ready for bed. I'm not sure about other single parents but for me it was pretty much wake up, get ready for work then get my daughter ready for school. While she was at school, I went to work. Once off work I would pick her up from afterschool then we headed home for me to cook dinner. We ate dinner, she did her homework, if she had any, then it was bath time and then to bed. Most nights we both were in the bed by 9:00 p.m. Every day it was the same thing over and over again just to pay the bills. There wasn't any joy to life - just work. Trying to do this thing called life.

This one day when I woke up in the morning it was just the same as any other day but what I did not know was that this would be the very day that would be the start of a life changing experience. It would be the day when I had to face the pain that I was carrying. I would have to take a look at life and realize that in order to have change you must be willing to make changes. You have to be willing to do something different to create change. I was working as a cashier when in walked a divine appointment from God. To this day I cannot tell you if it was a female or male. It was just a person off the street who spoke these words to me then walked out of the gas station. "You are blaming God for everything that has happened in your life". I responded, "No, I am not". Then off the person went and twenty five years later I have never seen that person again. For a few days I dwelled on what was said to me. Then came that day when I heard He Never Left Me on the radio. Over and over I played that in my mind, you are blaming God for everything that has happened in your life. Over, over and over I heard those words. I began to realize that yes I was blaming God. I was blaming God for my Granddaddy dying, and for my step Dad's actions with him putting his hands in areas of my body that he was not supposed to touch. So many things wrong in my life and yet I choose to blame God and not take any responsibility for any of them. How could that be that I would do that? How was I blaming God? I really didn't understand it at the time but the more I thought about it the more I could see that I really was blaming God for everything. It showed in my life as a Christian. That's just it, I was a Christian but one without a relationship with Jesus. I knew who He was and talked to Him about all my problems and cried a lot saying if you love me then how or why did you allow this or that to happen.

Gee, I had so much stuff going on inside I was like a walking time bomb ready to explode on the inside. Looking at me from the outside you would not know all this was going on inside of me but God knew.

At that time in my life I was at the lowest that a person could go. Even though I had been through and done a lot of things losing my Granddaddy was especially heart breaking to me. Deep down inside I was really mad and hurt that God had not listened to my prayer to let my Granddaddy live as I watched them do CPR trying to get his pulse back. I had buried that pain down deep just like I had done with so many things. Then at the right time, just as God's timing is always the right timing, I heard a song over the radio. He never left me song by Quinton Mills.

Chorus:
He never left me though I turned my back on Him living in a world of sin trying to run away again He

never left me when I chose to walk away. Even when I couldn't pray He never left me

Verse 1

So many directions the roads looked the same He gave me instructions

I disregarded in shame then sudden destruction soon came my way

I'll have to say I've got me to blame

Verse 2

I chose the wrong road. It looked good to me I walked blindly onward

I just could not see I was lost and I was dying But now I'm trying

You see I reached out to Jesus. You know he reached out to me.

As I listened to that song I cried, oh how it really touched me. I went and bought the cassette and once I got home I listened to it over and over. That song really ministered to my heart. Heart felt words he never turned his back on me though I turned my back on him. Wow so powerful and yet so true in my life. God never ever turned his back on me but I did Him. I did not want to have anything to do with God. I never told God to leave me alone because down deep in my heart I didn't want Him to leave me. I was afraid if he left he couldn't come back. I knew He was there I just didn't want to have any part of Him in my life. I knew that something had to change because I was completely wrong and missed having God active in my life. As I listened over and over to that song God told me to write letters to everyone who had hurt me. He was doing a work inside of me. After work there were many nights I laid across my bed and wrote letters after I laid my daughter down to sleep. I only wrote the letters when she was asleep or at her Dad's. I knew my heart would be torn open as I wrote and I did not want her to see me crying and asking a lot of questions as a seven year old would. It wasn't something I rushed through so it took me days to do all the letters. I wrote what came to my mind. So many memories, so many hurts, so much pain. I had held so much on the inside of me.

See, I was good at covering things up and walking away. I had gotten to be an expert at digging and burying things deep and pretending they are gone. If I did not want to think about something I could just push it to the side and leave it there. I just left it. Thinking if I did not think about it, it would leave. Not knowing enough about gardening, I convinced myself that just because I buried the hurts down deep in my heart they were gone. What was really happening was that the hurts were creating a root system that began to grow. Before I knew, it my heart was full of anger, bitterness, low self-esteem and many other things. But the fact is you may think the roots are gone or hidden but they always resurface and most of the time when you least expect them to and they can come out as angry eruptions.

My out of control point came after my Granddaddy had died and I was still recovering from being homeless and all the previous hurts. While at work someone said something to me and I grabbed them and pushed them up against the wall. My manager came out and got me then I quit and walked out the door. As I was walking, my manager was coming after me telling me not to quit just get some help with all the stuff I had going on. I didn't listen and continued to live what I call life. What is life? For me it was waking up every day and doing the same thing hoping and praying I would die so I could leave this world. If I had not been raised to believe that if you take your own life you would go to hell, I would have done so. To this day, I believe with all my heart, God allowed me to believe that just to keep me here on this earth. I sure didn't want to go to hell. I knew what I was living was already hell but the real hell would be a lot worse so I just lived life. I remember the times when I cried so hard I did not think I could cry anymore, yet more tears came. I did not want to live anymore, I wanted to die. I was ready to go I had failed at everything in my life, even trying to raise my Daughter. I was done and ready to check out of this world. As I wrote the letters I could feel the pain coming up and out of me. I only had one true friend. I pretty much shut people out of my life because I did not want to get hurt. In my so called life when I started opening up and allowing someone to get to know me they would do something to hurt me and then I would shut down again. I was a MESS on the inside and no one knew it but me and God.

Then that one day, "You are blaming God for everything that has happened in your life". Then that song, "He Never Left Me". Then that thought of writing letters. Why would I write a letter? That sounded just stupid to me! What good is that going to do? Why waste my time? I'm tired. I work, take care of my Daughter, and go to church. I don't have time to write letters. It came to that right time when I knew that I knew I had to write a letter. Then one letter turned into many letters. As I wrote, I cried and cried. I couldn't explain what was going on but something was happening to me on the inside. It was like I was crying all the pain out of me. How could that be? I spent hours and hours of writing and crying. How in the world can one person have so much stuff in their heart? A heart is not that big to hold everything I had coming out, but I tell you it was oceans of tears bringing the hurt and brokenness out of me. It was during this time when God was talking to me about my life and how holding on to the pain and hurt was also the same as holding on to unforgiveness. In order to be forgiven I had to forgive. I had said that I had forgiven myself and I did with words but I really had buried it down deep and left it there. Forgiveness really is a heart matter and comes from the heart. Once you truly forgive someone you will not hold on to the pain anymore. You don't get bad emotions when you're speaking about it. I knew I needed the real forgiveness for these people and I was finally ready to do it right. I always started each letter with "Dear" then I would say you have hurt me and I explained to each person how they hurt me. At the end I always said in order for me to go on with my life I must forgive you. I forgive you.

God told me to burn the letters when I was finished writing them. No one was going to see them so I was able to pour my heart out and be honest in each letter. Once I finished writing all the letters I took them outside and burned them. As they were burning the smoke went up as if it was going to God, so I was giving all the pain and hurt to Him. Not one person ever got the letter from me. It wasn't about the person I was writing the letter to it was about releasing the pain and hurt I had carried all the years. The letters below are not the original letters I wrote but samples of what the letters may have been like. Of course there were many more people than these few.

Dear Mom,
You have really hurt me

1. You hurt me by not being a Mom to me while I was growing up and not being there for me. I felt all alone in my life. I really needed you but you were not there. I would love to have talked to you about how things were going in school and if I did this or that, but, Mom all you cared about was your soap opera and soft drinks.

2. You made me feel like I was nothing and I was in your way. I felt like I couldn't do anything right in your eyes. I watched how you loved and cared for my brother but not me. Did you think I didn't need love or hugs? Instead I was given belt whippings so hard they left marks on my body. Even when I tried my best it was wrong in your eyes.

3. Mom, it tore me apart when you stopped talking to Grandma because you were upset when we spent time together. I remember the time she told me I had to go back home because you would not talk to her. Mom, do you not know that a person can love more than one person at a time?

4. Mom, you rocked my world when you handed me a hand full of pills and told me to take them. Mom, did you really hate me so much you wanted me to die, Mom? How could it be you carried me in your stomach and felt me kick and then you turned your back on me.

5. Mom, he was your husband not mine. Why did you let him treat me that way? Did you love him so much that you would allow him to do the things he

did to your first born, your only Daughter. Why, Mom, why? If you really didn't know it was going on when I told you, why did you asked me to leave the house not him?

6. Mom, was it because I reminded you so much of my "real" Dad that it reminded you of the pain of your divorce? Mom, what was it about me that caused you to hate me so much, Mom?

Mom, in order to go on with my life I must forgive you so, I forgive you with everything in my heart. I FORGIVE YOU!

Dear Daddy (my biological Dad)

You have hurt me Daddy,
I don't know what happened or why you and Mom divorced when I was real young. I cannot remember us living together because I was too young to do so. Daddy it hurt me with you not being in my life. Why did you choose to divorce me when you and Momma got a divorce? Do you know how much I wanted to talk to you, to spend time

with you but you were not there? Daddy I love you, you are my Daddy, and I am your only child. Why don't you love me? Did you not want me, Daddy? I have a void in my life and in my heart because you were not in my life. The few times we did get to see each other I loved being with you. I loved riding in that 18 wheeler with you even though you scared the daylights out of me coming down that mountain!! Daddy, do you know one of the memories I have with you was when the trailer started leaking when it rained so you had to get it fixed. You took me to K-Mart to buy underwear because I didn't have enough with me. Why that memory? I don't know but I cherish that memory. Daddy, many times I would wonder why you would go years without calling me or coming to see me. Daddy, I loved you, I was your Daughter and looked a lot like you. Daddy, I missed you so much I often cried because you were not with me, Daddy. I love you. You being absent from my life really hurt me. Did you think because Momma remarried and I had a step Daddy that I did not need you in my life? Was that what it was Daddy? I know you did not know what he was doing to me Daddy because I know you would have done something about it and not covered your eyes like my Momma did. Daddy, I love you. Daddy, remember the time I found your number and called you and asked if I could come see you and you said yes. Then when I called two days later and the number had been changed. Daddy that hurt me so bad I did not want anything from you just to see you, you are my Daddy and I am your only child. I feel like if you had known who I had become Daddy, you would be proud of me, Daddy. I have a lot of you in me, Daddy I drive for a living also, yes I have a CDL, Daddy. I often thought about you while I am driving and it puts a smile on my face. Daddy, I love you, I miss you and I wish you would find me or I could find you. I would love to see you and talk to you. Daddy I love you.

Daddy, you really did not do anything to me to hurt me but by you just being absent from my life hurt me. I have to forgive you for me to be able to go on with my life. Daddy, I forgive you and love you. Your only child, your daughter.

Dear Men,

All you men who have took advantage of me as a child and young teen and who caused deep wounds in me. You hurt me to what I thought was beyond repair. You knew what you were doing was wrong and the fear you put in me if I told someone. You broke my heart with the things you did to me. You took something from me that could never be replaced. I wasn't able to live a normal childhood because you took that away from me. What you did was create something in me that caused me to use sex to try to find love. As an adult I realized that I have to forgive you. Even though I think you may not deserve to be forgiven I still have to. I forgive you with everything in me and all my heart. I forgive you.

Dear Daddy (step)

How could you? You were married to my Mom! The times she sent you to pick me up from school or you told her you would pick me up and then you made that stop along the way home. How could you? The times you would come to wake me up in the morning by feeling my body right in front of Momma how could you? You hurt me so bad, the man who I called Daddy. The one who worked many hours to pay the rent, put food on the table, and you did that to me! I trusted you but you turned my trust into hate. I hated to walk out of school and see that big blue truck sitting there. Then the times you and Mom fought and you would hit her and her you. Then the time I said I was going to call 911 and you turned the kitchen table over on me. I hated you and wanted you to die. That is how much you hurt me. In order for me to go on with my life I must forgive you. I forgive you.

Dear Babysitter's husband

How and why would you touch a very young girl while your wife was sitting in the living room? I went to the kitchen to get something and you followed behind me. You are one lucky man that I didn't tell anyone but then again why would I and who would believe such a young child. You hurt me and you degraded your wife by touching me. You were the first one that ever touched me in a wrong way. In order for me to go on with my life I must forgive you. I forgive you. Even though I don't remember your name or what you look like I forgive you. That duplex was tore down to make a new road.

Dear step Daddy's brother

What was it that you saw in such a young child that you would want to touch me in that area. You asked me to get you something to drink and when I did you touched me. You were my uncle and you did that to me. You hurt me and I never wanted to see you again. No, I didn't tell Momma or Daddy (step). Would they believe me? Probably not. I carried what you did as a secret for many, many years and nobody ever knew but you and me. In order for me to go on with my life I must forgive you. I forgive you.

Dear Aunt's boyfriend

Did you not think I didn't know the difference between real money and fake? Why would you want to offer me fake money to do something to me? I ran for my life trying to get away from you and I remember it just as clear as if it happened right now. I sure am glad there was a dog in the house that crapped on the floor. You stepped right in it in the dining room and fell. Had you not you might have just caught me. I didn't have to tell anybody what you did Momma and Daddy (step) walked in right when it was going on. Did you like being handcuffed? You would have been in jail longer but Mom dropped the charges on you because she wouldn't let me tell the Judge what you had done. Your name is one that I have never forgotten. You hurt me that day and not only hurt me you, scared me. You caused me to not like men at all and the very thing Daddy (step) got mad at you about is the very thing that he started doing to me a few years later. You caused double pain in me. In order for me to go on with my life I must forgive you. I forgive you.

Dear Candy store man

If there was one good thing about you is I don't remember anything except walking in the store and you taking me to the back room. Other than that I don't remember. I was only seven maybe just turned eight and you did what you did. I never spoke a word of what you did and for some reason I blocked it all out of my mind. Whoever you are and where you may be I must forgive you. So with these words I forgive you.

Dear Roger,

Where do I even begin with you? Why did you drag me from outside to the bedroom while your wife was not there? I never thought you would ever do that to me. It was bad enough getting it from Daddy (step) and then when I finally told Momma about him she got mad. Momma called you to ask you to look at my car because it was not running right. See Daddy (step) had used the bribe of I'll will fix your car if you let me. I trusted you and trusted Momma on the way to your house that you would look at my car and fix it or tell me what was wrong with it. You were someone I looked up to along with your wife. How could you? I remember you hurt me really bad when you did it. I remember leaving your house. I was supposed to spend the night with Grandma and Granddaddy that night. I had to drive by their house leaving your house and I called them and told them I wasn't coming over. I drove home crying. You really hurt me and I felt really dirty to. When I got home I took a shower trying to wash you off of me. You hurt me! I was so scared to tell anyone I didn't think anyone would believe me. I was 16 and I remember. I didn't want to hurt your wife either. I loved her and trusted her. You hurt me and I lost trust in all men because of you. I loved you guys and you crushed that love. I missed time spending with my Grandparents because of you! I hated you very much and wished you would have died. You hurt me! I said that day when I left your house if another man touched me in a place I did not want to be touched, I would kill them. Let me say this, I meant it to. I am thankful you were the last one who ever touched me in that way. Thankfully, I did not have to go to jail for murder! In order for me to go on with my life, I must forgive you. I forgive you.

Dear Boss,

You hurt me in so many ways. The many times you called me into your office for this or that. The times you wrote me up because of another person. You, yes you, tried to crush every ounce of who I was. You made my time working under you very hard even to the point I hated to go to work! The time you told me "you don't get it". The time you tried to make me accept the responsibly of another person's actions. I could tell you never cared too much for me. You didn't have to say it your actions spoke louder than your words. The time I came to you with situations and you could not even respect me enough to look at me instead of your laptop. Once I got home from work there were many nights I cried my eyes out to God about how you treated me. You are a Christian man and wow is all I can say. Needless to say, I must forgive you and I do. I pray for you.

Dear Tamara (self),

I forgive you for thinking you deserve everything that has happened to you. I forgive you for thinking it was your fault that men touched you because you wore shorts. Tamara, I forgive you for thinking you could use sex to try to find love. Tamara, I forgive you for all the drinking and the drugs that you did trying to cover up the things in your life. Tamara, I forgive you. (I can assure you the real letter was much longer than this sample!)

Dear God,

Please forgive me for thinking that everything in my life that was done to me, you allowed. God, forgive me for all the times I asked you if you loved me and why did you allow the things to happen. God, all the times I sat under our trailer in my young teenage years just talking to you, believing that you really did not love me, God, please forgive me. God, please forgive me for choosing to drink and get drunk, have sex and to do drugs trying to cover up the pain in my life. God, I realize now that everything is not from you and people have a free will and do things they know they are not supposed to do. God, please forgive me for all these years having resentment towards you and for turning my back on you and believing that you were not there for me. God, forgive me for thinking that I would never be good enough for you to love me and even hear my prayers. God, forgive me for believing that I must be good and do good works for you to even love me. God, I know now and God, thanks for being there and holding my hand when all this junk was going on. God, I love you.

To this day I still write and burn letters to release the pain and hurt. I never want to be a person who does not forgive.

12.
Holy Spirit Heal the Memories

It wasn't until 2012 when I heard the voice of Holy Spirit say, "Heal the Memories". I did not have a clue to what it meant. I was in an inner healing class where we sat in group like settings and talked about our pain and hurts in our life. During this time of discussing our hurts we prayed and asked God to heal our hearts. Years back I had done a lot of forgiving of past hurts and wounds but I still had some memories. When I would think about the memory in most cases it was associated with pain and I could feel the pain still there. I had rededicated my life back to God in 2010 after that very heartbreaking divorce in 2005. When I got married in 2003 I really thought it was for the rest of my life. I had waited seventeen years after the divorce from my daughter's Dad because I wanted to make sure it was going to be real and last. After he left the marriage in July, 2004, I was devastated. I was told by several people at my church that I had "missed God" and should not have married my soon to be ex-husband. I thought if I had really missed God on that then what else had I missed God on?

While I left the church we were attending at the time, I did not turn my back on God. I still talked and prayed to God but our relationship was not a close one. It was more like a long distance relationship. I didn't talk or pray to God every day; just now and then. I also didn't go to church and at that time I did not want to have anything to do with a church.

Thankfully, that has changed and I am a member of an awesome church. I am active in my church and growing in the Lord. I had signed up for the inner healing class because I wanted to be able to help others who were at places that I had been. God had been using me to minister to others; however, I had not had any formal training other than Holy Spirit teaching me along the way. In this class the leader spoke about times in our lives when we are going through storms or had something happen and we still carry the pain and hurt of that situation. More often than not, we wonder where God was during those times. During the class I started thinking about my own life and the times that were still a little hurtful to me. I had forgiven my step Dad for the stuff that he had done and that released the pain of him rejecting me. But what I was finding was I still had some memories that were very painful to me. I remember the times in my Mom and Dad's bed, the times he picked me up from high school and the side road he always made a pit stop. Even though I had forgiven my step Dad, the memory was still painful for me to remember. So many memories and so much pain associated with the actions of the person I had forgiven. But why did I still have the pain in my memories when I had forgiven the people? It was not until I was able to see Jesus at that time in my life, in each memory, did I know that I was not alone and He was with me. As God would bring a memory back to me, it usually had pain with it and I had gotten to a place in my life and with God that I knew that the reason that memory was coming back, was because God wanted to heal the memory so I could release the pain associated with it.

In my earlier years, before I had gone through the healing, I had asked God, if you love me why did you allow that to happen? Why didn't you stop him from doing that to me? It was at that time that God spoke the truth to me and taught me about life. God is not a God who can change a person's free will but he can change a person's heart. Proverbs 21:1, "The king's heart is in the hand of the Lord, like the rivers of water He turns it wherever He wishes." When God created humans He also placed inside them a free will. Every individual has access to their free will whether it is right or wrong. Everyone knows the difference between right and wrong. When a person chooses against what they know is right, they are doing so in their free will. God told me the things that happened to me were not of His choice nor His will. While things happened He was not able to stop it because the people were acting in their free will. During this time He did not leave me. He was there the whole time holding my hand. So when these things were happening to me it was not God's fault nor did He approve it. Quite the opposite if you want to know the truth. Once I got ahold of that in my heart it changed my mindset.

Okay, back to the class. During the class a memory popped up in my thoughts. I was thinking, why am I thinking about this? As the class went along I found that when Holy Spirit brings a memory back to our remembrance, he wants to heal that memory. So as I thought about that memory of my step Dad pulling off the road in that big blue truck and doing his free will to my body, I asked Jesus, "Jesus where were you when this happened?" He showed me He was right there beside me holding my hand. He couldn't stop it because my step Dad was operating in his own free will and he knew what he was doing was wrong. Then as the class taught me to do, I said Holy Spirit heal that memory. Then when I thought about that memory again it did not have any pain associated with it. In class I learned the steps. They are:

1. Ask Holy Spirit for a memory that he wants to heal.
2. Once you get the memory - what is the emotion(s) you feel?
3. Ask Jesus to show you where He is in the memory.
4. Ask Holy Spirit to heal the memory.
5. Go back to the memory and see how you feel.

Once you forgive a person, it does not mean your memory is always healed, of that situation. Once your memory is healed when you are looking back at that memory you should be able to remember the memory but not feel any pain, much like a scar on your body from a cut. When you look at that scar you can remember how it happened but you can hit that scar all you want and you will never feel that pain again. Why? It is healed completely.

Over the years Holy Spirit had bought to my memory lots of memories. I was driving home from cleaning a house on I-85 in North Carolina and out of the blue a memory popped up in my mind about the day I was at my Daddy's house packing my things to come back to North Carolina. I was crushed and heartbroken and yes, driving down the highway while all of this was going through my mind. I just simply spoke these words Jesus, show me where you are in this memory and there He was sitting on the bed with me. He was there and then I asked "please heal the memory". As soon as I said that I felt a peace when I was thinking about the memory, healed. Thank God. This was around 2013 when this memory came back to my memory and that situation with my Daddy had happened in 1987. Wow, so far back and yet it must have been really important and deep down for Holy Spirit to bring that back to my remembrance, so it would be healed. Not all memories that pop into your memory are memories that need to be healed. There are very good memories as well.

I recall waking up from a dream. I saw my ex-husband sitting in a chair. I knew God was telling me there was something that was still inside me that I needed to forgive this man. Not sure, what it was I said the words, I forgive you for everything including the things I may not remember. I had forgiven him for several things; however, I believe sometimes you may need to forgive a person more than once for different actions against you. That day was the last time God brought my ex-husband back to my remembrance.

If a memory comes to you that has a negative emotion such as anger, pain, and anxiety etc., the chances are very good Holy Spirit brought that memory to your remembrance to bring healing into that place of pain. When this happens, just simply ask Jesus to show you where He is and then once you see Him ask Holy Spirit to heal that memory. You should have a peace and/or no negative feelings after it's healed. I found that during this time in my life. I still had memories that were associated with pain. Many were so far back in my younger years that I had forgotten them. Forgotten in the natural but still locked inside the painful emotions. It wasn't until I had received inner healing and was healed of the memories that I was really free from those situations.

13.
A Love Not Worth Finding

Growing up I wasn't the one that was given a lot of love or hugs or told I love you. It was a rare occasion when I heard I love you from my Mom. My Grandparents, on the other hand, I knew, they loved me beyond words could ever say. They supported me and if I had a problem I could always go to them. It seemed the older I got the more my Mom distanced herself from my Grandma. I believe it came from her being jealous of the relationship I had with Grandma. It seemed the talks with Grandma would always end with, "I can't tell you what to do", even when she wouldn't or couldn't give me advice, I knew she loved me.   And I was the apple of Granddaddy's eye.

In spite of the love from my Grandparents, I still got the wrong perception of what love was because of the abuse that I encountered/endured. I knew how to spell it and knew what I felt like it should be but I never knew real love growing up. Maybe that came from the absence of my biological Dad and being sexually assaulted so many times that it allowed that dreadful orphan spirit to overpower me.

Around the age of 16, I slowly got to where I started having sex with guys thinking if I did they would love me. In and out of relationships at such a young age I was really just trying to find what I thought was love. To me sex meant a way a person loves you. I had many boyfriends in my younger years, many one night stands just trying so hard to find that love that I so wanted. Time after time I found I was not able to find love. So I used the bottle to cover up things. Everyone loves a happy drunk right?

While I was in the world, I was trying to find what real love was in all the wrong places. For me, it was hanging out at the bars having drinks and dating guys. I used to think that one day I would find love. Years ago I heard a song "When We Make Love" by Alabama. The song made me think about "making love" verses just sex. I believe "making love" would be when two people who were in love came together in the bed. In my life it was never that but taking your clothes off, "getting it on" then getting it done. Nothing but sex no love involved. My whole life seemed to be like that thinking that giving a man sex would eventually turn into love.

Fast forward several years later when I met a guy. We just met and started doing a few things together such as camping, fishing and drinking. Then came the day that forever changed my life, we were in a car accident and I almost died in the accident. We were going down Highway 40 and got hit from behind twice by the same car. That caused the truck to start flipping and we went airborne across the highway to hit another car then went over that car and hit another car and then we landed upside right in the grass. As I was recovering from the accident and out of work we spent time together. He told me many times that I wasn't his type and he wasn't attracted to me but yet I still hung out with him. The more time we spent together the more my love grew for him. I tell you for the first time in my life I was really in love or should I say I thought I was in love. My heart just melted when he called or whenever I would see him. Even though he had his girlfriends and he would call to talk to me about their problems I still loved him. Fast forward again to the day I walked down the aisle to marry the love of my life on April 4, 2003. During the dress rehearsal I almost called the wedding off because I had an uneasy feeling and did not want to go through with it. I had been divorced for 17 years and I was at a good age, 39 to get remarried. My daughter was a teenager and did not require me to take care of her. I had been divorced for 17 years so I felt I was ready to remarry but I really had the worst uneasy feeling and wanted to call it off at dress rehearsal but did not. I already had all the dresses, sent out the invites, and had the cake made. I loved this man. He was the very air that I breathed. He was everything to me.

Fast forward again to 14 months later when I came home to find he was moving out. Things were not good in the house. There was a lot of fighting between him and his son and it caused us to argue as well. Heartbroken is not the word that would describe how I felt. I was devastated. I wanted to kill him so bad! My pain was deeper than I had ever experienced. I was beyond mad that he would refinance my house then leave the marriage. I had agreed in December 2003, to refinance my house to help him get out of debt. I did not know that he was in a HUGE amount of debt. I knew some. I was thinking maybe a couple of thousand dollars' worth of the debt. But on April 13, 2003, I asked him as we were going to see about filing bankruptcy. Now note, that is only nine days after we got married. That was the day I found out he was over $100,000.00 in credit card debt. Before I married him my house payoff was $69,000.00 and when he left July 2, 2004, it was $132,000.00. He knew I used the settlement from the accident to buy my house so I had a lot of equity. Not only was it about my house, it was also that I got married on my Grandparent's wedding date. Then I watched the man who I truly loved leave. It bought a lot of pain from the past. It seemed everything that I loved always left. To be honest, I felt like it would have been a lot easier had he died instead of leaving the marriage. At least if he had died, I wouldn't be facing the rejection again in my life. I wanted to crawl under my house and die. For five years after he left, I carried that pain and hurt and I knew that I had to forgive him no matter what. I had walked away from the church and pretty much done my own thing. I cried and cried, it seemed like for years. Then one day I realized I had to have a talk with God. Oh it had been so long and my pain was so, so deep.

Again God did a mighty work in me and it started with forgiveness. It was during this time that God started showing me that what I had really felt with this guy was not love but unhealthy soul ties. When you are intimate with a man (a soul tie can be created with anyone you are sexually active with) it creates an unhealthy emotional bond between the two of you. For my ex-husband, the fact that we almost died together in the car accident also contributed to the bond (soul tie) we had to each other. The accident created a bond between our hearts and a soul tie.

Once God started showing me and teaching me about soul ties and what they were, I realized that I really did not love my ex-husband but rather it was a soul tie. The feelings of love I felt were false feelings of love. That's why I called this a love not worth finding. It was during this time when God started healing me of the spirit of rejection and the orphan spirit. God showed me because of my biological Dad not being a part of my life it created a spirit of rejection in me. I felt my Dad had rejected me. God also showed me that I had an orphan spirit because I felt everyone always left me or abandoned me. I had to renounce the spirit of rejection and accept the spirit of acceptance. I also had to renounce the orphan spirit and receive the spirit of adoption. Once that junk in my truck was gone then I was able to accept the love of Jesus and I was able to love him back. That's when my life really took a turn for God. When a person has never been loved, doesn't know what love is, and has not been able to receive love, then you usually cannot accept that Jesus loves you. That was a life changing experience and one that I needed and it completely turned my life and my relationship with Jesus around. That's also the time I was able to love myself and to see myself as Jesus sees me.

Once God had done a mighty work in me, I went from knowing the name of Jesus and just a conversation to having a relationship with him. To me, my relationship with Jesus, is knowing that I have Him as a friend and He is always there for me to talk to. It does not matter what time or where I am, Jesus is always there for me to just talk to. I talk to Him just as I would my best friend here on earth. I also have this way of thinking that it is okay to tell Jesus what I really feel because He already knows what is on my mind and heart. So why hold anything back if He already knows? The inner healing brought me to a new level, a new me, and a new oneness with Jesus. That's when I found what true love was and I was able to accept His love and to be able to truly love Him back. Now when I say "I love you" to someone, it's not just words but it's from my heart. I really do love you. That kind of love is worth finding.

14.
Double Rainbows

It's was 1990 when I was really sick. I had given up my apartment because I was not able to pay the rent. I tried to work but kept getting fired for being out sick. In that year alone I had 13 jobs. I was trying my best to raise my young Daughter and deal with sickness. It was June 1990, when I was rushed back to the ER. Duke ER knew me very well from being there often. Spinal taps and all kinds of test were done over the past couple of months. Doctor's ruled out all sort of things and they finally came to the conclusion that I had cirrhosis of the liver. When I was told that, I just couldn't imagine that being true since I had stopped drinking years ago. At that time I barely drank at all.

I was driving to work just trying to make that dollar when the pain hit me as hard as it had time and time again. I was in huge amounts of pain and could not drive even the last mile or so to my Mom's. I pulled over and called her from the payphone and she called 911 for me. I had to leave my car and I made that trip to the ER again in an ambulance. That one visit would be the one that would completely turn my dying body around to being alive again. This one doctor who I had never seen told me I do not think you have cirrhosis of the liver, I believe it is your gallbladder. He ran tests and they came back positive for gallstones. I had so many of them that they were back into the vile of the liver causing it to back up into my body. This is what was causing my liver to shut down. Even the white of my eyes were already turning yellow. Folks, I was checking out of this world and there was nothing I could do to stop it.

At that time I was not at a place with God to even cry out for my life. The doctor wanted to do emergency surgery on me but was not able to. Point blank I was told I would not pull through so they were going to admit me in the hospital to get me built up enough to do the surgery. While filling out the paper work they brought me orange juice and bananas. All along my Mom was talking to the hospital staff about me going home because I had a small Daughter. They agreed to let me leave and come back in two days for the surgery. I was thankful to be able to go home (to my Mom's because I had lost everything at that time) to see my Daughter just in case. I didn't want to die but I knew the truth and I knew how bad my health was.

I didn't try to make it right with God because I didn't feel it was right to do so because I was on my death bed.

Two days later, on the way to the hospital that morning was the beginning of a little I love you from God and Him saying everything is going to be okay. I had seen a double rainbow for the first time in my life. I knew that I knew I would live through the surgery. I just knew it. I knew God was saying you are going to be okay. I knew this was something special from God. That was the beginning of the double rainbows. I am so thankful for that double rainbow and I remember that still 28 years later the peace that came over me when I had seen that double rainbow. On the way to the hospital I kept focused on what I had seen and knew enough about God to know He was with me. I came through and was told as soon as the gallbladder was removed my liver would start functioning again. From that time it seemed that when I was facing something in my life that was really hard, God always gave me a double rainbow. Even at times when there had been no rain.

I will only talk about a few of the times that stood out more than others. I remember right after I went to work for the school system in 2005 after the heartbreaking divorce. I did not know that the last few months before he left, he had not paid the bills at the house or the mortgage. Everything was in my name as he moved in with me. I trusted this man and believed that he was taking care of the bills as I added my income into our joint account. He asked me to watch his youngest son and he left the house. After being gone just a few hours he came home to tell me he had closed our joint bank account. I had been working part time cleaning houses while married so I could take care of his three boys. Right after he left, my house had gone into foreclosure. During this time I did not know what I was going to do. It seemed the harder I worked the more I got behind and was not able to catch things up. I didn't waste money or spend it on unnecessary items. Everything I made went to bills but there was not enough to pay all the bills. I was on my way home from work one day and I knew my house was almost close to the sell date for the foreclosure. I looked up to the sky and there it was a, double rainbow. I was blown away. It had not even been raining! Again, I knew that I knew God was saying everything was going to be okay. See, I still had not been through all the inner healing so hearing God's voice was a little hard for me. So He gave me something I could see with my own eyes and when I had seen the double rainbow it bought peace over me as it was a sign that it's all going to be okay. Sure enough, everything was okay and it's been 13 years and I am still living in my house.

Now I am at a place with God that I can hear His voice very easily and I have a relationship with Him so I don't have to have double rainbows like I used to in the past. I still go through hard times and trials but now it's my faith that gets me through instead of a double rainbow. However, God still surprises me with a double rainbow at times.

I had a job that allowed me to drive brand new school buses right off the manufactures parking lot straight to the buyer. I drove across the USA and Canada delivering school buses. In June 2016, oh my, oh my, did I make a mistake. I was in an intersection moving real slowly to see if the other three buses made it through or not. As I was looking in my side mirror I saw a white truck hit the side of the bus, a brand new $100.000.00 bus I was driving! A lot of damage was done to the side of the bus! I was scared and in shock. I was in Canada and I had never had an at fault accident in the 35 years of driving. I wasn't even at home or near being home. The police came to the accident and questioned me. I thought the white truck had run the red light but I ended up getting the ticket for disobeying a red light. I knew I had not run the red light but was going very slowly through the intersection when it turned red. One thing you do not do is argue with a Canadian police officer while in Canada. I needed my passport to stay open to enter into Canada. I had no clue as to what was going to happen to my CDL. I had been driving 35 years and had a clean driving record. The week before, I had gotten a speeding ticket in my car. I had a ticket 16 years earlier and that was all I had ever gotten on my CDL or driver license. The ticket was one week to the day the wreck happened. I tell you, I felt like I was going to have a panic attack, I was so scared! What was I going to do if I lost my CDL? All I know how to do is drive. What was I going to do?

I talked to God about this; I cried out to God. The speeding ticket, yes, I knew I was speeding. I was trying to get to work on time. I own that but this wreck was an accident. Would I be able to still come to Canada? Would I still be able to work this summer job driving? Would I lose my job with Department of

Public Schools which was my fulltime job? These were questions I did not have the answers to.

After all the paper work and including a ticket, I drove the bus away from the accident and my mind was all over the place. I was just trying to get to the motel for the night, deliver the bus the next morning and then get back to the USA and then finally, my home. I was over 2,000 miles from home. As I drove I looked up and caught the reflection of my cried out eyes in the rear view mirror. The whites of my eyes were so red and swollen from crying. Then there it was, in Canada, a rainbow. But a single rainbow was not my sign - it is a double rainbow. Just as I said, God that's a single one not double, there it was the second rainbow. It was a double rainbow! Now folks let me say if I ever needed it at a time in my life it was then. At this stage in my life, I knew God and I had a personal relationship. I knew His voice and knew He was with me but fear was trying to grip me. If I lost my CDL it took away my ability to pay my bills. When I had seen that double rainbow I knew that I knew everything would be okay.

When I got home from Canada I had a lot of letters from attorneys about my speeding ticket. As I called around I called this one office. I heard the Lord say they are Christian. I asked the young lady are you a Christian and she said "yes". I asked if the attorney was also a Christian and she said "yes". I said you are my attorney - God told me you are to be my attorney. So I hired them. The plus side he only charged for $49.99 where other attorneys' wanted way over $100.00. I told my attorney the truth that I knew I was speeding and was trying to get to work. I had stopped to get breakfast and it took 20 minutes and I had started to leave without eating but choose to stay to eat. The exact thing I told the police officers and I still got a ticket. He told me that because it had been so long since I got a ticket, he dropped it from 70 in a 55 to 64 in a 55 that way it would be under 10 miles over. I said thanks but I would have preferred a warning. I was up front and honest I did not lie I knew I was speeding. I asked the attorney to please try to get it dismissed and he was honest with me that really was pretty much impossible. I asked God for his mercy for my speeding ticket even though I knew what I was doing and still disobeyed the law. I was on my way to eat dinner with a friend in Raleigh and my heart was heavy with not knowing about the wreck in Canada and the speeding ticket and if I was going to lose my CDL. I was on Highway 540 in Durham NC and looked and there before my eyes was a double rainbow. I knew that everything was going to be just fine. I was rejoicing at that double rainbow.

Once I got to the restaurant I asked my friend did you see the double rainbow and she said no there was no rainbow there. But I had proof of the rainbow I had taken a picture of it because I was so excited over it. I was heading back to Canada when I found out while in Ohio at a truck stop on break that my speeding ticket was dismissed. The first thing I said was "thank you Jesus!" I heard my attorney laugh he knew it was only God! Then I told him how thankful I was and that I prayed I'd never have to have his service again. The accident in Canada NEVER showed up on my CDL or driving report, BUT GOD! I could name several more where God has giving me a double rainbow to let me know everything was going to be okay, but I'll end with this. Maybe you need a little encouraging. Maybe you are facing a hard time. Maybe you wish God would give you a double rainbow. Let me say that everyone is different and God speaks to all of us differently. Maybe your faith is enough for you so you don't need a physical sign. Or maybe you need a sign every hour. God is the same God for me that He is for you. He doesn't treat us any differently. He loves us all the same no matter where we have been or how long we have been with Him. He loves us. He chooses to show me double rainbows because I am a person that gets things through pictures more than just words. That's just how I am wired.

15.
HOLD ON!!!
This is going to hurt!!!!

November 22, 1999, I had taken the afternoon off from work and a friend and I were going shopping. We left his house and were heading to Chapel Hill to Linen and Things. It was a normal day warm outside and we were on Highway 40 in Durham, NC. I remember my friend say "HOLD ON"! I did not know why he said, "HOLD ON," but I knew by the tone of his voice it was NOT good.   The next thing I remember is seeing my daughter's face come before me and I said God don't let me die and leave her without a Momma! I don't know if I said it out loud or to myself. I feel like we must have been flipping because I remember I was bracing myself with my hand on the roof. I recall a woman coming up to me asking if I wanted her to call someone for me and I said yes, my Mom. Somehow I remembered her number! I also said I need water and she gave me her bottle of water. I noticed blood everywhere and asked whose blood, then I lost my vision. I wasn't able to see. I could hear the sirens in the distant. I heard we don't have time to life fight then I heard red and green codes. Someone came over to me to tell me they were getting my friend out first then going to use the Jaws of Life to get me out of the truck. I was also covered up to help protect me from the debris from cutting the truck. The noise was so loud and scary for a person that couldn't see. At this point I am in and out of consciousness so I only remember bits and pieces. I told them my leg was broken and I was going to die if they didn't get me out of the truck. They stopped the jaws-of-life and I wiggled to the door as they pulled me out a very small opening. I somehow knew that I was lying on the highway and I thought great I survived the wreck now someone is going to come run over me and I'm going to die! I did not realize the highway was closed in both directions.

I felt like I was going to fall off the bed in the ambulance they were going so fast. The siren was really loud. They were cutting my clothes off and I told them DO NOT CUT THE RINGS AROUND MY NECK! I had my Grandma's wedding rings on a chain around my neck. Once at the hospital I remember my Mom coming up to me and her hand over her mouth. She had just had her teeth pulled that day. I remember the pain I was in – it was unbearable. So many tests being done and the pain didn't let up. I had been in the emergency room for over 24 hours as they ran this test and that test. I had to have surgery on my leg. I knew my leg was broken but they had yet to put a brace or anything on it. My friends sister came in to see me and when she found out my leg still had not been braced or set she took care of the matter!

My injuries were numerous but I was alive! My left leg was broken in three places and needed surgery. My right shoulder was broken and needed surgery. My right leg went out the window while flipping and had road rash on it. My right arm also went out the window and there was a big hole all the way to the bone on my elbow. I had a bad closed head injury from my head hitting the payment while we flipped across Highway 40. My left wrist was broken and my right ankle. The last four vertebrae's in my lower back were broken as well. My left hand went out the sunroof while flipping and it also had road rash on it. The chief surgeon of Duke Hospital Sports Orthopedic told me I was a "train wreck and they had to put me back together". At some point while in the ER, I got my vision back. The whites of my eyes were red from the blood vessels busting from flipping. At the time I had no clue as to how bad the accident was. We got hit from behind then the same car hit us again. We started flipping side to side and crossed over the median on Highway 40. We hit another car then flipped over that and flipped nose to tail then hit another car and landed on all four tires.

It had been several days that I was not able to have food because I was bleeding internally and they were trying to find out where. I was hungry and I told the nurse if they did not give me something to eat I was going to call 911 to come get me to take me to Burger King! Well neither one happened. I kept seeing insects flying around me and nobody else saw them. People thought it was the drugs I was given that were causing me to see things. Turns out that I had floaters and the floaters were moving around looking like insects. I had never heard of floaters before and did not have them before the wreck.

After being in the hospital four days, on Thanksgiving morning I called my Grandma and told her to please call my Pastor. I knew I was dying from losing the blood and I needed prayer. Only by God's grace did I remember his number to give to Grandma. My family brought Thanksgiving dinner to the hospital to spend with me. My only request was Grandma's homemade banana pudding. My family got there and just as they walked in the door so did the nurse to take me for more tests. As they were rolling me out my Pastor walked in and prayed for me. Turns out I did not get a bite of that banana pudding!

The next morning I got the news that THE BLEEDING HAD STOPPED!!!!! That was an answer to prayer! The nurse rolled my bed down to see my friend only because I wouldn't stop asking about him. They opened his door and we had seen each other then they rolled me back to my room. My heart was at peace; at least I knew he was alive.

I had surgery on my leg and the physical therapist came to start working with me showing me how to use a walker and other things. My walker wasn't a normal one. It had an arm rest on the right side because my shoulder was broken and I could not use my hand to hold on. The left side had a peg like thing because that wrist was broke.

Life was really hard. I was used to taking care of myself and now I could not do anything for myself. I could not wash, brush my hair or teeth. I could not even wipe myself after using the bathroom. You talk about losing all sense of pride and being humbled. My daughter and her friends took care of me.

I slept in the lazboy once I went home from the hospital. That was the only place I could keep my leg and shoulder elevated. I was in pain and decided to do something stupid! My daughter was asleep and I didn't want to wake her up. She had helped me so much! I tried to put the lazboy down so I could get up. The only thing I did was turn that thing over on the side! Now you are talking about a mess. I was in a mess! Now I had no choice. I was waking my daughter up by the loud noise coming out of my mouth from the pain I was in!

A couple of days after coming home from the hospital my daughter went back to school. My Aunt told me about a lawyer so I called him. He was coming over that day to see me. I was able to get from the chair to the wheelchair alone so I felt I could be left alone for my daughter to go back to school. I had to take my medicine so I got myself into the kitchen. Then it happened I got stuck! I could not move the wheelchair the foot pegs were dug into one side of the cabinets and the back part of the other side. No phone, no one to hear me yell. I was stuck! Then my lawyer knocked on the door and I yelled for him to come in. Leaving the door unlocked was a lot easier than trying to get to the door to unlock it. He helped get me out and made me a sandwich so I could take my medicine.

I stared feeling like someone was going to break in my house and kill me. I was diagnosed with Post Traumatic Stress Disorder (PTSD). I had to go on the medicine to help me. I took it for a few weeks and then took myself off of it. I did not like how it made me feel.

As time went by my body started healing. The physical therapist and the nurse were no longer coming to the house. I was getting around in the wheelchair pretty good and my in home physical therapy insurance was coming to an end. I had to buy a different car an automatic and four door. I had to go to the doctor every day and needed to be able to drive myself and carry my wheelchair. Thankfully it was my left leg that broke and not the right so I could drive!

I remember going into the elevator at the doctor's office to find that the door started shutting before I could roll myself all the way in. There I was, the door kept trying to close and was banging on the wheelchair. I was stuck and I could not roll myself in or out! Again, no one was there to help. Then finally someone came to my rescue!

That wheelchair caused me a lot of trouble and a lot of laughter as well. My friend, Tim, came and got me to take me to Northgate Mall to buy my daughter something for Christmas. We went into a store and I realize I could not get to the area I needed to because I was in a wheelchair. I was so upset. It took a lot for me to be able to get out of the house. I had this cooler with ice in it that had hoses connected to it and the Velcro wrap on my shoulder. It pumped ice cold water to keep the swelling down. I also had to get several pain pills in me as well. We ended up leaving the store and the mall without what I went to get. As Tim was rolling me out the door there it went. The wheel broke off of the wheelchair! Now I was in a bad mess. I couldn't walk nor put pressure on that leg. To be honest I don't remember how I got to the car but I got home in one piece.

My days were filled with doctor's appointments. This time I heard the words your bone is not growing back and we are going to have to do a bone graph. I didn't know what that was but I knew I did not want it. The Doctors gave it just a few more days to see if it would start healing. At my next appointment my Doctor decided to use an electric bone stimulator (I forgot the real name). It sends shock waves to the bone. This was the last attempt before a bone graph. The machine that I had to wear would send shock waves to the bone. I also went back into surgery to remove the lower screws around my ankle. Finally the bone stared growing back together!!! Another answer to prayer! I was so tired of surgeries I had five within 10 months.

Then it was time to start walking again. That was so, so hard! Walking is something you just do, you don't think about it. I tried and tired and could not get it.

My brain could not tell my foot to move back and forth. I was giving up and said I don't know if I will ever walk again. Then one day, a friend who was a former Marine stood behind me as I tried to walk with my walker. He yelled toes heal, toes heal, and toes heal. He stayed right in behind me yelling with that Marine voice. The more he yelled the more I was able to connect the two. I started walking with my walker.

It was hard getting use to my new life. Life was not the same as it was before the wreck. I was not able to do a lot of things that I used to. Because of all the surgeries and all the pain I ended up getting hooked on pain pills. It took me until 2003 to get off of them completely. My memory was the hardest. It took a big hit and I lost a lot of memories. To this day I still don't remember things. It's funny how our brain will remember some things and not others. I still have floaters from time to time.

It's been 18 years now and I have adjusted to the "new" life. I went back to work to find that my brain would no longer allow me to do the job that I once did. I put my notice in and started cleaning houses. Something that did not require me to use my brain/memory and I could work at my own pace, one that my body would allow me to work.

I did have a lawsuit to cover my injuries. I used my settlement to buy my house. My attorney used his $89,000.00 to buy himself a BMW. Yes, that is what he got from my case.

I believe with all my heart the real reason I survived that wreck was because I cried out to God "God don't let me die and leave her without a Moma". I know that I know the reason I was able to pull through all the months of pain and everything associated with the wreck was God. He was there to help me; He was there to comfort me. I wasn't alone.

The driver of the car was a 20 year old guy with three teenage passengers who were also under the age of 20. I was told they had been at a bar all night and he had fallen asleep at the wheel. The wreck happened at 2:10 p.m. so the time frame did not seem right to me.

The driver did not have a driver's license and it was not his car. The car belonged to one of the passengers who let the young man drive. The police found cocaine and a case of beer in the car. Neither the driver nor the other teenagers were ever arrested; even though they should have been because they were underage to buy beer plus they had the cocaine. I was able to make it to all the court hearings even though I was in the wheelchair only to hear it was postponed time after time. At the last court hearing the young man's lawyer told the judge there was enough car insurance to cover the accident. The judge ordered the young man to pay a $50.00 fine and the cost of the court!

Unbelievable, to this day that is all the young man got. The truth was, there was not enough insurance money to cover everything. You cannot put a money price on all my injuries. By the way I will never forget that young man's name!

Months later after the settlement was over I called the witness that was on the police report. One was a truck driver who told me he almost wrecked his 18 wheeler by locking up his breaks to put the truck in both lanes to stop traffic from hitting us again. Once our truck came to a rest he moved his truck to the side of the road. He told me all he seen was all my body limbs coming out the windows as we flipped. He also called the hospital to see if I lived and was told yes. Of course that was before all the new privacy laws. I talked to the daughter of the man driving the car we hit and flipped over. He was an older man and had to have stiches in his head. He was afraid of driving after the accident but was okay.

My heart did not want to forgive this young man at all. He forever changed my life. He took away things that I loved doing and would never be able to do again. Riding roller coasters came to an end that day. After the accident, my daughter and I went to an amusement park and we rode a roller-coaster. I got such a headache and was not able to get rid of it. I finally had to go back to my doctor. My doctor told me that my brain was scrambled in the wreck and my brain could not handle riding a roller coaster with all the jerking. That was one thing I loved to do, but now I am not able to do it. To this day I still have sharp shooting pains running through my head and the back of my head tingles and will go numb at times. It only lasts a few seconds; however, when it does it HURTS! I still have some memory loss as there are a lot of things I don't remember from before the wreck. There are times I have problems remembering things just a few hours later. Often times, my daughter and I will have a conversation and I may not remember that particular time or that particular situation. But I could tell you that I am alive, able to hold down a job and I'm able to pay my bills. I'm can function as a normal human being. I will say that is only because of God!

I'll be honest; it took a lot for me to get to where I could forgive this young man. In the past I had emotional pain and physical. This was different. This was physical pain and I would even say torture to my body. God keep speaking to me and helping me to be able to forgive the young man and the police officer who did not arrest the driver. At first I did not want to listen to God or obey. I wanted justice! I thought he should do jail time or something. He did almost kill us by a careless act. As time went by, God won the battle and He walked me through forgiving this young man!

Around the end of July or the first part of August 2012, God told me I needed to renounce the lies. I didn't understand what He was talking about so I questioned what it was that I was to do and He told me to renounce the lies spoken over my body. I really didn't understand. Then He started to explain the words spoken to me after the wreck. That once a bone is broken it will never be the same. Renounce the lie of when a bone breaks you get arthritis. I had been living in pain for the past 13 years because of all the injuries from the wreck. I'd done everything He told me to do by renouncing the lies and not believing what I was told. It was at that time God gave me a vision of my feet in the water at Moravian Falls, North Carolina. From what I understood, it wasn't until I renounced the lies that God was able to heal me. There were times I was hardly able to walk and I was on daily pain medicine. I told one of my friends about the vision and she invited me to go with her and her family to their Mountain house and Virginia. We would take a trip down to Moravian Falls as well. As soon as we got to Moravian Falls I took my shoes off and I walked in the shallow part of the water. I want you to know that was the last day that I took any pain medicine for all the injuries from the wreck! God healed me that day.

I don't know why He chose the way that He did for me to be healed. Or why I was to go to Moravian Falls and put my feet in the water. I wasn't quite sure of why I needed to go but I kind of felt like that would be when my healing would take place. It was never proven by a doctor; however, I believed that I did have fibromyalgia prior to the trip. I know that I know it wasn't until I stopped believing the lies that God was able heal me. Whose report are you going to believe? I will believe the report of the Lord that I am healed.

WARNING: IF I AM EVER IN THE CAR WITH YOU DO NOT TELL ME TO "HOLD ON"!!!! YOU JUST MAY SEE ME JUMPING OUT OF THE CAR. How do I know this? Ask the person who told me to hold on years after the accident. I went to open the door. Those words sound an alarm off in my head!

Just recently, February 18, 2019, during water aerobics God told me you are no longer a victim. To be honest this is one that He had to explain to me. He took me back to November 22, 1999, when the car accident happened. Ever since that day I have always said "I almost died in a car wreck". Not realizing it, I was placing more emphasis on the accident that almost killed me and not the fact I had lived. He told me to start saying I am a survivor of a bad car accident. See that changes things from death to life, from negative to positive. I really had not thought about the accident that way. Once I made the word change it changed something inside of me. So often we speak and we don't realize the power of how we word our words.

16.
Grandma's Final Gift

My boss had sent a co-worker to the school to get me and bought a substitute driver to take over my route after the phone call from my Grandma's nursing home. On the ride back to the compound I called the funeral home to go get my ladybug. They asked if I wanted to go see her one last time and I said no. I am a firm believer that when you take your last breath you are no longer in that body and it's just a body. I had no need to go see her body. I had left nothing unsaid or unresolved with my Grandma, so I didn't need to say a final good bye. I called my Daughter and told her and then called my Uncle so he could tell my Aunt. The office staff offered to drive me home but I said no. I only lived four miles away and I was okay. In shock, but okay. Grandma was 91 and had a wonderful life and now she was with Jesus and my Granddaddy. What an awesome place to be.

My small family got together and went out to eat and discuss what needed to happen. The next day my Aunt and I went to the nursing home to get Grandma's things. We then went to the bank to close her account and then to take clothes to the funeral home. I choose to put a gown on her. I preferred to have her sleeping instead of all dressed up making her look dead. My mind stayed on not hearing my Grandma say I love you anymore. See my Grandparents were the only ones that showed me love and told me I love you. I knew that I would not hear those words again. Besides, who was going to pray for me now that she was gone? No one in my family went to church, much less pray.

My Aunt and I took off to my Mom's to get her to sign one of the policies and then grabbed some lunch and then went back to the funeral home to see Grandma. Once there they showed us to the room and there was my Ladybug all snug in her gown looking a lot better than she did two days before she relocated. I was shocked by how good she looked! Then I saw a teddy bear sitting on her heart leaning up against the back of the casket. It had on a pink shirt with UNC (University of North Carolina) on it. My Aunt jokingly said "that's not mine it yours." She is a huge Duke fan and I am a UNC fan. I knew that was not Grandma's so I took it out and gave it back to the funeral home.

The next day the funeral home told me they called the nursing home and that bear was in fact Grandma's. A nurse had given it to her and she had died with it in her arms. Wow, is all I can say. This is what the Lord spoke to me about the bear. The bear was a Madagascar bear which is in Africa and God had spoken to me three years before that He was sending me to Africa. It had a pink tee shirt on and pink was my favorite color. UNC all the way for me. Then God brought it all the way home speaking to me about this little bear. God used a nurse that would hear and OBEY his voice to buy that bear. He instructed what bear to get and she listened. The undertaker came to get Grandma and God made sure the one that was sent would hear God's voice to pick up that bear. They usually only get the body and nothing more. Then the person who dressed my Grandma also heard His voice to put that bear in with Grandma. Then God and only God would make sure that everyone knew that bear was for me by it being pink and UNC. See, only God could do that. Why would He do that? Because He loves me so much and knew I needed something just a little extra. God put the people in the right place at the right time that He knew would hear His voice and obey. He did not leave anything undone and He did this all for me because He loves me so much and wanted to show me how much Grandma loved me. Let me tell you I knew that woman loved me. No doubt in my mind! That's why I call that bear Grandma's Final Gift and it was all done out of love from my Heavenly Daddy.

Two years later, from the time I was planning Grandma's services, I was in Africa on a mission's trip. If God had not called her home I would not have been able to go on the mission trip. God spoke to me a month before my Grandma died that He was going to be calling her home. I was okay with it because I knew that I knew she was ready and never wanted to live in the condition that she had gotten. Grandma's final gift and a little praying bear I received from my physical therapist who worked with me after the car accident are in a plastic zip bag sitting on the top of my dresser in my bedroom. Life does go on after losing a loved one. The best thing is when you know Jesus, and serve Him you know you will see them again. A few weeks after Grandma relocated to heaven I was talking to a friend and as we were talking God gave me a vision. I was standing far off and I could see the gate in heaven. At that gate was my Granddaddy. He didn't look like he did here on earth but I knew it was him. He was looking to his right and I was to his left. He didn't see me or look my way. His eyes were set to the right. Then I saw my Grandma walk up to that gate where he was standing. I don't know how the gate opened I didn't see that part. I saw them take hands and walk into heaven. My Grandpa was walking perfectly. Here on earth he had a wooden (back then they were wooden not metal) leg because he had cancer in one of his legs and had to have it removed. That vision will forever be in my memory and I am thankful God loves me so much and gave me another little gift in the form of that vision. Maybe it was Granddaddy wanting me to know - hey thanks for taking care of your Grandma for 22 years 11 months and 6 days. You rest now, I will take over. By the way we love you and we will be waiting for you to join us.

17.
He Loved Me Enough To Send Me Crutches

February 10, 2018, while at Catch the Fire church (CTF) during worship with the song, Oh How He Loves Us, I saw Jesus come up and blow on my face. I knew He was blowing in a refreshing wind on and over me. He told me that I am not alone and the reason I made it was he was in my Mom's womb talking to me. She had six miscarriages before me. Then I remembered the vision I had of us dancing together kind of like a slow dance with a blue dress on and it blowing in the wind. Then I was reminded of the vision I had when Jesus and I walked beside the Sea of Galilee holding hands. He was pointing things out showing me what He wanted me to see. Then He showed me during the hard times in my life He sent someone to me to help me get through. He called these people crutches. Crutches help hold you up when you are not able to walk alone. Most of the times He sent friends who I had not seen or heard from in years. During my teenage years I had a friend named Terri. She had come through some of the stuff that I had as well. She remained my friend even during the times of drinking, drugs trying to cover up the pain deep inside and what was going on.

In 1989 when my liver was shutting down, I became homeless with my daughter because I was not able to work. A friend out of the blue, so I thought called. He found out what was going on and he came and got my daughter and me. Every morning he would take us to a friend's house to help watch me while he worked. After work he came picked us up and took us to his house. Many nights he cooked dinner or took us out to eat. He helped care for me and my daughter. Because of him we had a bed to sleep in and the same place every night.

October 16, 1990, my Granddaddy dying right in front of me, was probably the hardest day in my life even to this day. While at the hospital trying to overcome the words "I'm sorry" my cell phone rang. It was Larry who I had not heard from in about a year or so. This is the same guy who helped take care of me when I was sick. I told him Granddaddy died. He came to the hospital to get me and take me back home to my Grandparents. He was there for me during that time when I needed someone to hug me tight! The last time I heard from Larry was January 2001, and again I needed help. This time it was different I was still recovering from the wreck and had bought a house and needed to move from my apartment to my house. I was not physically able to move things. It seemed that every time I heard from Larry I was going through something!

November 22, 1999, I was in a really bad car wreck. I don't remember much but what I do remember is a woman talking to me. I wasn't able to see because the blood vessels in my eyes busted leaving me without sight. She asked if she could call anyone for me and I said yes my Mom. To this day I don't know why I said my Mom instead of my Grandma unless it was because my Mom didn't live too far from where the accident happened. I also remember telling her I needed water. She told me she had a bottle of water but had drink out of it. I said okay and took the bottle of water. I just needed a sip of water for some unknown reason. I don't know who that woman was at all and never got to say thank you or see what she looked like. During the time of the accident I did not drink water, soft drinks was my drink. I also did I drink after anyone and still don't not even my daughter. For me to take a bottle of water and drink after someone my body must have needed it very bad!

July 2, 2004, was the day my ex-husband left. Folks let me say, it took the breath out of my body when he walked out that door!!!! Out of the blue again a friend, Tim, called. I had not heard from Tim in years!!!! He came over to the house and got me. He took me to Walmart and then to have a few drinks. He helped ease the pain and mainly calmed me down from calling all my friend's asking if I could borrow their gun! He just may be the one that God used to keep me from going to jail for attempted murder! At that time I did not know how to shoot a gun it would be attempted murder. Now I know how to hit the target, it would be murder.

Why am I saying all of this? It's for this reason so many years so many times we walk this life and we think that we are alone. Yes, Jesus is always with us but there are times when we need someone in person to help us. I never really thought about how God will send us a crutch to help us stand up. The more I look back at my life and the times I came through things, I see where God sent someone to keep me standing. Maybe they're only meant to be in your life for a day or two, maybe a season I don't know. I think He used different crutches for different things. Ask God to take you back through your life and show you the times He sent a crutch to you. It will change you no doubt.

18.
Year Of Jubilee

April 18, 2014, was going to be one awesome day in my life. It was Good Friday and the day that I was to turn 50. Way before the day even came; I started declaring that it would be a year of jubilee for me. Not just my 50th year but the entire 10 years until I turned 60. I knew that I knew God had chosen the right time - His time for me to be born. I also knew that it was God not by chance I turned 50, on Good Friday. I knew that it was going to be important. I declared that great things would happen and doors would be opened. I would also be repaid seven times what was stolen from me. Not long after I turned 50 my house came out of foreclosure. That right there was nothing but God. I tell you the mortgage company came after me hard every time I got behind. I believe that it was the enemy trying to take away what God had given me. The very house that I used to associate with almost dying became a blessing. The same house that God spoke to me about over and over; even giving me a double rainbow as a sign that I would not lose my house. I had to stay strong and keep the faith in terms of what God had told me.

It was around the end of 2010 when God told me He was going to send me to Africa. It wasn't until October 2014, that I went. I had tried to go several times before but the door was never opened for me to go. God saw to it that it would happen in His timing and it would be in what I called my year of Jubilee.

In 2010, my employer closed one of the divisions and I was transferred to another division. People there really didn't care too much for me. I stayed in trouble all the time, getting written up as well. I was written up more in the eight years being at the division than my whole entire working life. My hours were cut from eight hours a day to four to five. I wasn't bringing in enough money to pay my mortgage or make my car payment, so I had no choice but to turn in my car. I kept applying for jobs and would never hear back even with 35 years of driving and a clean driving and background record. I finally accepted that God wanted to me to stay where I was. For five years I drove old cars with high mileage so I would not have a car payment. I never complained. I was just happy to have a car to get back and forth to work. It was April 2018, when God opened a door me for to get another job. It was totally God, how everything worked out. I would work less hours and make more money. Finally I was able to keep up the yard, the house and work and it did not take a toll on me. I needed a new car for this job due to mine having 172,000 miles on it. I found a car online and went to the dealership to buy it. It was a 2015 with 59,000 miles on it. I stopped by the dealership to look at it and to my surprise I was able to be financed for the car. I had been on a long journey with my credit, almost losing everything, then trying to rebuild it so I knew my credit score wasn't great. It had been ten years plus since I bought a car and I did not realize that 16.9% was very HIGH. As I drove home I felt like God was giving me back what I had to turn in. I noticed the transmission seem to be changing hard and slipping. I called the dealership and was told the car didn't have 100,000 miles on it so it shouldn't be the transmission. They said it had the new CVT transmissions and I probably didn't know how to drive the car since my old car was a 2006. Instead of believing in myself, I took them at their word to find only to my car being towed in September 2018. The transmission had gone out! I went back and forth with the manufacture and ended up getting the transmission rebuilt at a big price of $4,100.00. Thank God the manufacturer paid 70% leaving me 30% or $1,100.00. Ouch that hurt! Then three months later the transmission started slipping again at 16,000 miles! After a week, I started going back and forth with the dealership that rebuilt the transmission. I waited every day for the phone call to let me know what was going to happen. The Sunday before, I had seen a vision of a mountain and the dealership name written on the mountain. I watched as the mountain crumbled before my eyes. I knew

God had this! The following Friday I was told my claim was denied and I could not get help with the new transmission that was also going to cost $4,400.00. I was very upset and not sure what to do. I didn't have the money to fix it again and who is to say that it wouldn't go out again. My only choice, I thought was to turn it back in to the creditor which I didn't want to do. I have worked so hard on rebuilding my credit. I called another local dealership to see if there was a general manager over that dealership in Durham that I could talk to and they put me on hold. I hung up and then called another one. I was connected to a man named Rob. As I told him my story I cried more and more. I had no clue as to what to do. I still owed $10,500.00 on that 2015 and I only had it for 10 months. The general manager told me to come in and see him. He wanted to see if he could do something to help me. I drove to the dealership thinking I might get help with the new transmission. BUT GOD HAD OTHER PLANS! Once there they could tell my eyes were red and swollen. I tried to hold it together. They sat me down and gave me a bottle of water. They asked for my information, such as my name and all that. They ran my credit and my score was 650. That wasn't a good score at all but coming from where I was, it was good. Then the salesman took me outside to look at new cars! I was told in order to get out of bad debt, I had to buy new to transfer the bad debt. They crunched a lot of numbers and gave me $6,000.00 for my car! It was the same manufacturer and as everyone said they had never heard of a transmission going out twice. This dealership was really trying to help me! I test drove a car and decided that was the one. I wasn't trying to spend a lot of money. I needed to get out of the car that I was in and have something that I could depend on. I was told I was going to get an 11% interest rate and was okay with that. It was 5% lower than what I had. I stepped outside and my salesman was coming toward me in a car and it's not the blue car I was buying. He told me he wanted me to see this particular car because it was an upgrade from the blue one and had all the bells and whistles. Before I even looked at it I asked how much he said "same price". They were upgrading me free! I looked at the car and said let's sign! I didn't even test drive that car.

It was a 2019 with only five miles on it. I had never had a brand new car! I called a friend who lived in the area to see if he could meet me at the dealership. I just needed to run all this by a friend to make sure I was doing right. Once there he told me to try to finance it with my bank to see if I could get it lower. Knowing my credit score I really didn't think that would happen. I asked him what he had and he said a 3% loan. When signing the paperwork the finance officer said I gave you a 3.9% finance rate because "I like you". I was like wow! I keep saying am I really driving that car from here? Am I really getting that car? I thought they were going to change their mind while signing the paperwork. I had been on the new job 10 months and I knew my credit and where I was coming from. I just could not believe it!! I texted my friend to tell him I got a 3.9! I also got a 120,000-mile bumper to bumper warranty, including the transmission. After all the paperwork was done in the end it saved me a lot of money going from the 16.9% to 3.9% even on a new car, and canceling out the bad debt with a good one. Then four days later I got a call from the dealership. They changed my percent rate and I needed to come in sign the papers again. My heart sunk and I was like I have the paperwork with 3.9% I don't' have to sign again. I asked what the new percentage rate is. She told me she got me down to 2.9%! I said I am on my way! In the real world I should not have been able to buy that new car. I should not have gotten a 2.9% interest rate. That's in the real world, BUT with GOD all things are possible. I believe it is God honoring my year of Jubilee. He also gave me something I have never had, a brand new car. Oh by the way, the color of my car is gun metallic. My gun metallic car is used as a weapon for the Kingdom Of God. I use it to minister to others. The metallic is a grey color which is the color of a mountain. I believe the mountain I saw in the vision was the 2015 car crumbling into the 2019 vehicle. ONLY GOD can do something like this!

I had lost a lot in my lifetime and needed to be paid back a lot. The scriptures say we are to be paid back seven times what the enemy steals from us. He sure has a lot of paying back to me!

I also believed God would renew my relationship with my Mom and it would be restored and I'm still believing for it to happen.

I still walk in faith that the relationship with my "real" Dad will also be restored - not really restored but renewed. Why would I say that? Because for something to be restored, it must have existed before. My "real" Dad and I have never really had a relationship so it would have to be something new. I also believe my year of Jubilee would be a year that the dreams I've had would be refreshed and fulfilled in this season. I believe all the promises that God has spoken to me over the years will be fulfilled in my life during this season of Jubilee of my life.

Of course I am not without heartache even in a year of Jubilee. Losing my Grandma was a huge stab to my heart but then I have to look at the fact she lived to be 91 and had an awesome life.

And of course there are bumps in the road. I guess going from a Tamara mindset to a year of Jubilee mindset changed everything in me. Maybe, just maybe, it's me that has truly changed because I believe in a different way. Now I trust more because it is a year of Jubilee. I have always said, God, I don't know how but I know you will work this out. I may not see how you are going to do it, but I trust you. I tell you, everything always works out! It may not turn out the way I thought it was going to but, it always works out.

I cannot put my trust in men, only in my God. The God who created this world. The God who formed me in my Mother's womb. The God who sent His Son to the Cross for my sins. The Son who said IT IS FINISHED. The God who raised His Son from the grave. In this year of Jubilee I have learned how to live my life according to the word of God. IT IS FINISHED. When Jesus said that, I believe it and I live it. IT IS FINISHED! When I say IT IS FINISHED I mean everything that I face in my life from day to day Jesus went to the Cross for. There is nothing the Cross does not cover.

19.
The Cross

August 5, 2011, I was going to a church in Highpoint, North Carolina, that I had never been to for the Friday night service. I knew something great was going to happen because God was sending me there and I had no clue as to why. Three days before I left, Holy Spirit told me to get re-baptized before I go to Highpoint. See I had been baptized but not since I stopped smoking several years back. And get this, it had to be where fish swim which meant not a pool. Several of my friends agreed to baptize me in Falls Lake. We also took communion afterwards right in the parking lot at Falls Lake!

I had been asking God to make the Cross "real" in my life. I knew about the Cross and all the details, I just wanted it to be real in my life. I wanted it to move from knowledge in my mind to real in my heart.

That night while at church during worship I was standing with my eyes closed, just worshipping. As I worshipped, God took me to a place I had never been before. He gave me a vision but this time I was in the vision. It was much like I was watching a movie and I was in it. I was walking down a dry and dusty area. It wasn't a road but like a field or something. Then in the distance I could see the Cross as I got closer I could see Jesus on the Cross. When I got about two feet from the Cross I could see Jesus' blood running down His body and dripping on the ground. I heard the voice of God "you are standing on Holy Ground" I knew it was the blood that made where I was standing Holy. As I got a little closer, my eyes went from the ground moving up Jesus' body. As I got about to his stomach area, I reached in and touched His blood. I got blood on my finger tips and I rubbed it in between my fingers. It was wet and warm, meaning it was alive! Then my eyes moved up to his face area and as a blind person would do to someone I put both my hands on His face and patted around His face to feel His face. His eyes were open and He didn't say a word as I loved on my Jesus. I could see all the blood coming from the crown on His head and the love in His eyes. As my eyes moved to the top of His head the position of Him changed so that He was laying on His back on the ground with the Cross under Him. He was about at my mid-section height. His arms were still on the Cross and the crown was removed. I could see the holes in His head from the thorns and the blood coming out. I put a finger in one of the holes and it was warm, full of blood and about two inches deep. Then in a very soft, full of love voice, Jesus said, "Does this bother you?"

Folks, that day the Cross became really real in my life as never before! God answered my prayer. I don't know if anyone has seen me with my hands patting Jesus face or rubbing His blood or if I was just in the spirit at the Cross. I don't even know how long I was there. What I do know is I was still standing in the same place and they were still worshipping when I opened my eyes.

On February 2, 2013, I was getting to leave for two amazing services. I was at home crying out for healing for a friend who had been given two months to live. I was crying from my inner parts claiming the blood of Jesus on and over her. Then I started asking Jesus "What was it that kept you on the Cross when I know you felt the pain of that hammer and nails?" At that time, I was taken back to the Cross and I saw Jesus on the Cross yelling out to the crowd "I LOVE YOU, I LOVE YOU," that is all He kept saying over and over while He was looking at the very people who put Him on the Cross and to the ones who didn't believe in him. Then I said "God what was it that kept you from coming from Heaven to help your Son?" "I know you saw His pain and hurt." Then I saw God sitting in Heaven with a host of Angels ministering to Him.

My life has never been the same since these two visions. In the past I knew Jesus and who he was but now I have a personal relationship with Him. He has become my best friend. That is also the day that I realized how much He really did love me. It wasn't just words written in the Bible anymore.

Since that day there has not and will not be any turning back. Seeing that Cross changed my life. I tell so many people that I have come too far now to turn back. A lot of things that I used to do are no longer a part of my life. I don't miss them at all! I am a new woman changed by the power of the Cross.

Psalm 34:8
Taste and see that the LORD is good; blessed is the one who takes refuge in Him.

20.
Wouldn't Change A Thing

So many times I've been asked, what would you change in your life if you could? My answer has always been the same for years. I would not change anything except maybe refinancing my house to help my ex-husband. But I still would have married him.

It's obvious that I have been down a lot of roads in my lifetime. Some that I did not choose, some I did. Each road that I traveled, there was a lesson to be learned or forgiveness that needed to occur. It was the very roads that I took, broken or not, that lead me to where I am today. Many of the roads I had to crawl down because the pain was too heavy or the burden was way too hard. There have been times when I did not think that I would make it but I had to keep going. I had a child who needed her Mom and to be honest - I had a Grandma that needed me also. God made me a fighter and one that does not give up. It's because He knew before I was born I was going to need extra strength to be a fighter. I will say this, after the birth of my Daughter; I never thought about taking my life again because I had a reason to live.

I remember a time, years and years back, when as a young adult I said some things and at the time I really did not know that God would take the words I said to heart and do it! I meant the words to a point, but not to the extent of where it ended up taking me. I said "God shake me and break me and make me into what you want me to be." Little did I know the number of things that I was going to face to get me to the shaking and breaking. It was during this time that I was as low as low could be and all I could do is say God, Your will not my will. God, I give you my whole life, not just a part. It was during this time when all hell was coming against me that I could see Jesus moving and changing things in my life.

I'm reminded of a vision God gave me years back of how wine is made. The vineyard must be pruned removing the dead stuff away. Then the grapes must be picked and crushed in order to get the grape juice. Then the grapes go through a filter. The filter removes everything, only allowing the grape juice to flow through. Then the juice is placed in barrels and placed in a cold dark cellar for a period of time. I could relate this so much to my life and how after a time in the cellar the grape juice is turned into wine and is ready for everyone to enjoy. Had the grapes not been pruned there would be no wine. Had the grapes not been crushed there would be no wine. Had the juice not been filtered removing all the junk it would be useless as wine. Had the grape juice escaped the dark cellar while waiting for it to mature, the wine would not be as good. Wow my life was compared to a good glass of wine, and I don't even like drinking wine! See God had to take the stuff out of me in order for me to listen to Him. Once everything was removed, I was able to hear God clearly and have a personal relationship with Him. It was during that time when I was able to really say, I love you God, I love you Jesus, and I love you Holy Spirit. That's the time when my life started becoming one with Jesus and I started walking by and being led by Holy Spirit.

A few years back God gave me a vision during worship at the church I was attending. I saw a small baby maybe five to six months old in a crib. God had an oil tin and was pouring anointing oil over the baby. He said there have been many roads you have been down that you thought were mistakes when in fact they were part of my plan for your life so you could be a more effective witness for me. That was the day when I realized that everything in my life was part of God's plan for my life. He did not cause the sexual molestation but it would be used for His glory. I'm able to talk to women who have been molested and tell them my story. Because I have been there, I understand the feelings that one carries inside and the shame and hurt that comes along with it. So many women like myself don't tell anyone when it happens to them. For me, it was about him hurting me or maybe killing me if I told. It was also, who would believe me. I also did not want people feeling sorry for me or shaming me.

I also remember a time I said there is not a situation I have not been through. Out of the mouth of a young woman who had no idea what she had spoken. It was not long after that I found myself sick and then homeless. If only I had not said that one sentence. One may say I spoke it into existence. But you know what since I have been homeless, now I can relate to people who are. Had I never been homeless I just might not be in a position of having compassion for the homeless. I tell you there is power in your words.

The broken roads in my life have developed a compassion for so many. I heard someone say your mess is your message and I believe that 100%. I do not like to see people walking in life feeling down and low about their selves or seeing people so negative and down all the time. I cannot stand to see someone mistreat another person or being mistreated.

My dream is to see people walking in their full destiny from God. Walking in a healthy relationship with God and loving their lives. The reality is not everyone will reach their full destiny, but I sure would like to see it happen. I would love for people to be healed of broken relationships and things that have happened to them. To walk in the fullness of life that God has called them, and be who God created them to be.

So I would not change anything in my life even if I could. Each and everything that has happened whether good or bad has put me at this time and this place in my life. I believe that I am where I am to be and doing what I am to do. It took years and years to get here but I am here. My life is not over, I still have things to accomplish in my life.

I pray that my life story, in return is able to help someone who may have gone through similar things. If my life is an open book, perhaps it will help someone else and it will all be worth it to me. Because of God helping me to forgive so many people, I am able to live a life full of joy and use my life as a testimony for God. The road of forgiveness was not an easy one but one I had to do. It's not easy to walk back through your life and a life of hurtful memories so you can begin to be healed. But the end results are more than words can describe.

To be free of the pain, to be free of the hurt, nothing can compare to that. There is only one healer and His name is Jesus. Drugs, alcohol, sex and other worldly things cannot heal the pain, it only covers it up. In due time, all the substances and things will run out and you will find all the pain still there. If you really want all the pain and hurt gone - it takes Jesus. To be honest it hurts when you are being healed but once healed the pain is gone! It ripped my heart out as I wrote the letters. I cried buckets of tears yet while the tears were flowing - God's healing was coming in.

God,
I pray for each person that has read this book to come to know you as their Father. I pray that hearts will be healed and the broken things in their life be made whole through you.

I pray Ezekiel 36:26 (ESV) "And I will give you a new heart, and a new spirit I will put within you. And I will remove the heart of stone from your flesh and give you a heart of flesh."

God,

I pray that each person will come to know who they are in you and walk into what you have called them to be and do. I pray for lives to be transformed by the renewing of their minds. I pray that each and every person will come to a place where they submit to your will fully in their lives, not holding anything back.

Thank you, God for giving to me that I may give to others. Thank you, God that my life story will start a healing process in many.

In the name of Jesus I ask these things.
Thy Kingdom Come, They Will Be Done, On Earth, As It Is In Heaven for every person.

Revelation 12:11

"And they overcame him by the blood of the Lamb and by the word of their testimony, and they did not love their lives to the death."
The words written on these pages are just a part of my testimony.

With love,
Tamara J Aycock

Update on my Dad since the book was printed. I got call from my Mom on February 18, 2021 at 11:07 a.m. to call her, it was about my Dad. I knew that I knew and that is the day that the dream disappeared and the hope faded away. That "one day" would never come to pass as he took his last breath February 16, 2021 at 1:05 p.m. Just three days after his birthday.

Love you Dad!

My Grandparents
Warren and Lois Page.

My Grandma & Daughter
Notice her front tooth missing!

My Grandma & Daughter
Grandma's 90 birthday
8-20-2011

This cat came up to my Aunt and I when we were leaving the funeral home from making Grandma's final arrangements. Grandma had a cat Sweetie who she loved so much! This cat looked just like her cat Sweetie. It was a special moment for my Aunt and me.

Grandma's Cat Sweetie

The day my life completely changed. This truck is a 1999
Nissan Frontier Crew cab.
I SURVIVED!

Fulfilling the vision God gave me of my feet in the water at Moravian Falls. That day was the day God healed me!

No more pain pills, no more anti-inflammatory pills, no more pain. Nothing stronger than ibuprofen, except when I do a lot of hard labor such as yard work.

I don't know why God chose Moravian Falls to heal me but He did.